closer *still*

Scott Evans

To Mum and Dad.

For my inheritance.

First published by Hopefully Publishing

First Edition

Copyright © Scott Evans 2012

ISBN 978-0-9572622-0-1

Printed by Ross Print Services, Greystones, Co. Wicklow
www.rossprint.ie

Hopefully Publishing
Thornbank
Newcastle Road
Kilcoole
Co. Wicklow

www.closerstill.me
www.scottevans.ie
Cover Artwork by Scott Evans

Contents

The Easy Way   1

The Small Print   11

Why?   22

A Second Look   33

Of Two Sons   46

Home   57

Healing   69

Caught Kneeling   89

Twisted Questions,
Twisted Lives   104

Heroism   122

A Benediction   138

Acknowledgments

A few years ago, my Dad and I were driving up a country road near our family home and I was looking in at all the beautiful, incredibly expensive houses on each side. I asked him, 'Dad, if you hadn't quit that job and moved to Bangladesh, do you think we'd live in a house like this?'

Always quick to downplay the brave and beautiful choices that he and my Mum made in bringing us up, he replied, 'I don't know. But I do know that our time in Bangladesh and the ways in which it shaped you, that's your inheritance.'

That's why this book is dedicated to them. Mum, Dad, I love you both more than words can say. Thank you for showing us how to live and love well. At the end of my life, your lives will be the yardstick by which I measure my own.

To Tim and Linds, I am so lucky to have siblings that are also my best friends. You never fail to challenge me, encourage me, inspire me, believe in me, humble me and, most importantly, make me laugh. I love you both. To Kate, welcome to the family!

To Mattie, you've been there from the beginning. Nickel Brothers for life.

To Greg Fromholz, you have been one of the most important people in my life as my mentor for the last eight years. I am honoured to call you a friend.

To Jude Trenier, for taking a chance on an arrogant jackass like me.

To Bishop Michael Burrows, for your kindness, friendship and support. Looking forward to your book on Judas when you finally get it finished.

To Christina, Luke, Patrick, Chris, Russ, Ian, Alan, Dougie, Eoin, Joe, Alec, Gillian, Kaddl, Tim, Autumn and Willy. For your love, friendship, support and belief.

To the Elemental Team –Geraldine and Dee– for being crazy enough to join me on this journey.

To my young people. You have been one of the best things in my life over the last four years. You have restored my faith in the future of the church when I have begun to doubt it. Your questions, your honesty, your freshness, your madness are all why I love youth ministry and have been able to keep going for so long.

To Rob Bell (and Daryl Michael for introducing me to his podcasts in 2004) whose teaching has challenged, informed and inspired me through my iPod on road trips all over Ireland for the past eight years. So much of your teaching has shaped this book. I've tried to give you credit where I can but I'm sure you deserve more.

To Ian and Wendy Mullen and Lucy and Kieron Kelly from Ross Print Services. For all your work in getting this book printed and for your support and friendship throughout the process.

Finally, I owe a massive debt of gratitude to my editor, the unstoppable Simone Finney. You turned this book from a cumbersome rant into something I'm incredibly proud of. Thank you.

Chapter One

THE EASY WAY

Just Don't Do It ...

By my mid teens, if I was asked what a 'Christian' was, I would have answered that 'a Christian is someone who has accepted Jesus as their Lord and Saviour and doesn't get drunk, get high or get laid.' This probably hasn't been the case for everyone, but growing up in church taught me that a Christian was defined by what he or she didn't do.

Though I wasn't happy or inspired by it, I could live with this lifestyle because at least it was clear: it meant I got to go to heaven. It did, however, make sharing my faith pretty hard. Calling your teenage friends to a life of sobriety and chastity is difficult without some pretty serious perks in your favour. 'Heaven after you die' is the obvious one, but, according to my friends, it wasn't enough. Especially if Heaven is going to be a load of Christians sitting around for eternity continuing to not really do anything.

I can see where they're coming from. When you're not really convinced of something, it's hard to convince other people that you're right. And maybe that's the problem--I was trying to convince them that Christianity was right, not that Christ is beautiful or good.

Looking back on that time in my life, I can see why it was confusing to follow Jesus. On one hand, I have a very clear list of the things that a Christian does not do, while on the other, I had no idea who to be. It feels like being handed a map to the journey of life that has no destination, just loads of big red Xs marking the places you are not allowed to go to. Momentum becomes scary, our direction begins to be defined by avoidance and life becomes something to be survived rather than enjoyed. Some of us put our heads down and try to do just that. Others fall into the trap of shortcuts that we hope will help us figure out how to make it better.

The Easy Way

There's a temptation in life to pursue the quick fix. Whatever the problem is, we don't just want a solution; we want a solution that is quick, easy and affordable. Don't agree? Look at the adverts that we are constantly bombarded with. Radio ads about car loans being approved in 15 minutes over the phone, two-minute rice and 'The 60-Second Guide to Leadership.'

The really sad thing is that, even though I am so conscious of this, I'm among the worst offenders. I was looking for someone's number on my phone the other day when I found a hotline for six-second abs and considered calling it because, let's face it, we all want nice abs. But more than just wanting to look like we've been Photoshopped, it's actually about what I don't want. I don't want to do the work. I don't want to count the calories, cut down on soft drinks and fast food and I definitely don't want that desire to vomit that usual follows any significant effort at doing sit-ups. I really want the abs——just without the work.

It's true of my Christian life as well. I want the solution to the struggle I have with praying, an easy programme for reading my Bible and an alarm clock that will make me joyful about the idea of getting up for church. While these tools can work, they generally only transform my routine. They can get me on my knees to pray, but they can't force me to be intimate with God or hear His voice. They can transform my Bible reading patterns, but they can't make my Bible reading transform me. They can get my body to church, but they can't guarantee my heart will follow. Something else has to happen, something deeper than going through the motions.

I'm guessing that this is why Jesus did things the way He did. You don't find Jesus teaching seminars on living the religious life or releasing books called 'Praying the Jesus Way.' He doesn't zap people and make them good followers. He doesn't run a 'Day with Jesus' programme. He calls people——messy, broken, unreliable people——to follow

Him. And answering the call doesn't fix them; they don't just agree to follow Him and magically transform into the people He wants them to be. Even after He dies, rises and ascends, they're still broken, and they're still failing––but they are changing gradually. We were made for the tension, for the challenges, the journey––not just the destination.

Check it out for yourself. A year into following Jesus, James and John are asking permission to call down lightning on the unbelieving, Judas is stealing money from the community funds, and they're arguing as a group over who will be the greatest. Judas betrays Him, Peter denies Him, and when He's arrested they all run away. But Jesus doesn't rise from the dead with a list of dos and don'ts or a pamphlet on right living or a big stick to beat them with. He meets them on the beach, cooks them breakfast and gives them the chance to start again. The life of faith is not a five- or eight-step plan, it's a journey. It's got ups and downs, highs and lows, successes and failures, certainty and confusion, questions and answers, gold and dirt, blood and tears, heartbreak and healing.

We cannot pursue Christ by rote or formula or jumping through religious hoops. We must instead journey beyond knowing about Christ to knowing Him, from seeking examples of how to live to seeking encounters with His life.

Of Jesus, Wells and Serial Monogamists

I generally don't like passages that I've heard preached on a million times. It's like hearing a song or seeing an episode of The Simpsons one too many times: you lose interest and it loses its impact. The story of the Woman at the Well is one of those stories that used to send me to sleep when a preacher would ask us to 'turn in our Bibles to the fourth chapter of John.' Yeah, yeah, yeah, internal waters springing up to life eternal, water that satisfies, blah, blah, blah. And I hate referring to these passages because I feel like a walking cliché instead of someone who is 'cutting edge' (which is, let's face it, what every Christian communicator wants to be). But a deeper reason I don't like going to this passage is because it has been used for too long as 'the perfect illustration for evangelism':

1. Engage in a mundane conversation.

2. Turn the humdrum subject into the eternal.

3. Move the conversation partner to making a decision about accepting Jesus.

When we do this, we miss the depth of the passage, the beauty of the conversation and the heart of God expressed to someone hurting.

Forgive me if you already know the context of the passage, but it doesn't make any sense without it:

Jesus is at a well, where the women from the village would go together to get water for the day. They would go early, when the day was still cool, from the youngest to the oldest. It was a community event, a time to catch up on each other's lives, share news and gossip.

Jesus arrives at noon, long after all the women would have departed. Exhausted from the journey, He sends the disciples on ahead of him to the village to get food. He stops for a break ... and yet you can't help but feel there is a divine appointment happening here. It seems like an accident, a chance happening, but God is always doing something beneath the surface, something through us, in us or in spite of us, and this is no exception. Jesus meets this woman for a reason and the setting is important.

It's noon in Palestine (read: swelteringly hot) and she comes to the well by herself. 'Why come now? Why come alone?' John has his audience wondering. The readers know there is some deep or even dark reason, some secret, some skeleton in her closet, something that forced her out of her community, perhaps by the wish of others, perhaps self-inflicted, perhaps both. She comes as an outsider: excluded, isolated, shamed and ashamed. And this is where God in flesh meets her. A Jewish man starts a conversation with a rejected Samaritan woman, her race, her gender and her past all good reasons for Jesus to have nothing to do with her and yet He crosses each divide to speak deeply to her. She is astounded that He would even acknowledge her.

It begins innocently with a conversation about water, but very soon there is something deeper happening, another level at which they are communicating. The conversation comes to a head when He speaks of water that will never run out. But without the context, we can't understand what this truly means to her: This is not Jesus making her life more convenient like when I pray for a good parking space when I'm running late. This is a promise that she will never have to return to this place of shame.

The well is a constant reminder of whatever it was that drove her out, that forced her into loneliness, seclusion and abandonment, whatever it was that made her invisible, made her the talk of the Samaritan equivalent of the office water cooler or local pub. When she asks how she can receive it, Jesus says, 'Go get your husband.' It seems so random, almost misogynistic, but it is completely intentional. It is a guided arrow to the place of her deepest heartbreak and brokenness, to the external symptom of her internal struggle, her journey of finding her identity in the arms of lovers who hold the keys to the safe in which she will find her worth. Jesus indentifies her greatest vulnerability, and she responds in the same way that I've found so common to Christians in the 21st Century: 'I have no husband.'

Like Adam and Eve in the Garden, like we are all tempted to do when someone shines a light on our darkness, she hides. It's not a lie, but it's not the whole truth either. So Jesus, in order to heal her, reveals the whole truth, that she has had five husbands and the man she is with now is not one of them.

Many have called her the first evangelist because she then calls her whole village to come and meet Jesus, but she is also the first Christian. In reply to the spotlight Jesus turns on her wounds, she changes a conversation about her brokenness and healing into a theological debate about the proper place to worship. A conversation about life and how to find it becomes an argument about how to be religious.

This story is not a model for evangelism. The Gospels––and indeed the whole Gospel narrative–– cannot be reduced to a model or programme. It is instead a glimpse of the heart of God, a glimpse of ourselves and a glimpse of life. It is not Step One in 'The Jesus Guide to Conversion;' it is not prescriptive. Our tendency in processing this passage is to put ourselves in the shoes of Jesus, the shoes of the one bringing the news, to allow the words to transform the external manifestation of our faith when actually, we are the woman.

We are the one broken, the one with places of shame, the one with wounds to hide and fear of exposure.

The most common complaint that I hear about the Church and Christians is that we talk the talk but we don't walk the walk, that we aren't 'smoking what we're selling.' We––and I say 'we' because I mean me and others I know––want what the adverts and TV preachers promise. We want to reduce a lifelong journey to seven quick steps, to six-second abs, to microwaveable faith, to lose weight, feel great and be able to talk about Jesus and everything He 'offers' without having Jesus say 'Go get your husband.' It's time to turn from example to encounter, to put ourselves in the shoes of those who met Jesus, who were changed and are always changing, who were far away, moved closer and are always moving closer still: closer to Jesus, closer to life and closer to being the people that we were made to be.

Recovery and Re-Discovery:

If we are truly to figure out what it means to follow Jesus, we must stop defining our lives by what we don't do and stop trying to follow an example we haven't encountered.

If we are going to recover, we need to rediscover. Rediscover the heart of God. Rediscover the words and life of Jesus. Rediscover and even redefine what it means to be a Christian in our culture, our community, our world. We need to rediscover our faith as

'that something which you were born desiring, and which, beneath the flux of other desires and in all the momentary silences between the louder passions, night and day, year by year, from childhood to old age, you are looking for, watching for, listening for[.] You have never had it. All the things that have ever deeply possessed your soul have been but hints of it

– tantalizing glimpses, promises never quite fulfilled, echoes that died away just as they caught your ear. But if it should really become manifest – if there ever came an echo that did not die away but swelled into the sound itself – you would know it. Beyond all possibility of doubt you would say "Here at last is the thing I was made for."[1]

---

[1] From Chapter 10 of CS Lewis' *The Problem of Pain*. Just one of many passages and authors I was introduced to in Sean Mullan's Culture and Evangelism class in the Irish Bible Institute.

Chapter Two

THE SMALL PRINT

The struggle for me in trying to abandon the ways I've lived out Christianity in the past is that the 'Easy Way' is so much more attractive than an encounter with Jesus like the woman at the well. It's based on clear boundaries and expectations. If I pray this prayer, believe these things and abstain from this, this and that then I will be forgiven for my sins and go to Heaven when I die (or, sometimes more importantly, not go to Hell). Unspoken in this lifestyle is the belief that, if I hold up my end of the bargain, so will God. If I put this in, this is what I will get back. It's vending machine faith, a contractual agreement between us and the Almighty where everyone knows where they stand and what's required of them. To a certain extent, it's a trust in God to do right by us if we do right by Him. But another way of looking at it is a lack of trust of a God that we can't predict. We nail Him down to clear terms and conditions just in case He tries to change them and begins to ask for more than we are prepared to give.

Jesus tells a story about a nobleman who leaves his home to take royal power for himself. He gives three servants different amounts of money (called talents) to do business with while he is away. When he returns, he calls the servants and asks what they have done with what he gave them. As far as we know, he gave no instructions as to what to do with the money. He doesn't say to invest it in a particular place or to get a particular return for it. He just implies that they do something with it. There is no contract here. There is just an assumption that they are to take what they have been given and take a risk on it.

The first servant he asks replies that he invested the coin and made 10 more. So the master gives him authority over 10 cities. The second has made a further five and so is given five cities.

The third comes and says, 'Lord, here is your coin. I wrapped it up in a piece of cloth, for I was afraid of you, because you are a harsh man; you take what you did not deposit, and reap what you did not sow' (Luke 19:21).

I can only imagine the silence that falls over the room at that moment, the wincing of the first two servants as they realise what's about to happen and how foolish this servant is. What they saw as a blessing and a joy--their master's investment and faith in them--this third servant has called a burden, a test and an obligation. He's so afraid of losing it that he can't let go in order to invest it.

This is the danger of the easy way. It is often based on a belief in a harsh God who rewards inaction over risk and safety over danger. The easy way raises up Christians who are so afraid of being corrupted that their life cannot be contagious, who want the letter of the Law rather than the Law written on their hearts, who want to read the small print and ensure that they benefit from it before they commit to the life of faith.

As the old cliché goes, 'some Christians are so heavenly-minded that they are of no earthly use.' 'Easy Way' Christians scour the Scriptures for promises and commitments that remove all risk, needing the contract to guarantee that the life of faith will be a life without trouble, hardship or sacrifice. But they fail to realise that the greatest danger to them is the response of the master, who judges the third servant according to who the servant believes him to be.

It begs a couple of questions for us: 'What does the way I live out my faith say about who I believe God to be?' And 'What if He judged me according to the character I proclaim that he has?'

Promoting Christ with Cheesy Slogans and Half-Truths

I like to think that I am becoming more like Jesus. Don't get me wrong––no one's likely to call me Christlike any time soon unless they're talking about my beard and hair––but

I do have my moments when I look back and see that I am loving mercy and grace more. I realise that I'm finding the space in my heart for others that makes me more compassionate or that I'm building up the confidence to be more challenging.

Recently though, I've found myself more like Jesus when He quietly leaves the Temple, makes a whip out of cords and returns to the courts to clear people out with a justified, righteous anger. But it's hard to know if the feeling is really 'Christlike', as I hope, or if it's just me being overly sensitive and easily angered.

I'm not a violent guy, but there is an anger that rises up in me when I see my faith communicated in a way that is cheesy, over-simplified or watered down. It's particularly potent when I find myself at a Christian festival, watching people go by in Christian t-shirts. There is one that provokes such rage within me that it's all I can do not to tear the shirt from the wearer's body, set it alight in front of them and beat them with reeds until they promise to consult me on all future fashion choices.

The t-shirt features a big red button, the sort of thing you'd see in a nuclear bunker or space station, with 'Jesus' written on it. The caption says 'Push the button. It's that easy!'

Everything about it is wrong. The idea that pushing a button or praying a prayer makes you a Christian preaches that all Jesus wants is your acknowledgement, a tipping of the cap to His existence and sacrifice, and that your commitment to Him ends there. The promise that it's easy sets people up for a fall because, in my experience, following Jesus is hard, messy and confusing––and never claims to be anything else.

My problem with this t-shirt isn't just the shirt itself; it represents a bigger trap that many Christians and churches have fallen into. Living in an age of slick and engaging marketing, many congregations have become part of the branding machine, using every medium possible to communicate faith to the masses and draw them to Jesus. Many have failed to realise, however, that there is only so much that you can communicate on a billboard or t-shirt. You have to make a choice about the parts of our faith that you will promote, and the parts that you will leave out. The small print. The terms and conditions. In our effort to get people in the door, we have oversimplified the commitment, giving people false expectations of who Jesus is and the life He calls us to.

False Promises

Jeremiah 29:11 is quickly becoming my least favourite Bible verse. Some of that is due to its overuse. I see it written on Christian versions of Hallmark cards. I see it on posters with kittens. I work with teens and adults who cling to it as a central verse of their faith in tough times. I've heard it quoted so often that it borders on meaningless to me.

A few years ago I read the whole book of Jeremiah to get an idea of where it fits into his life and ministry to the nation of Israel. I came across something startling that I have hesitated to share with people because I don't want to burst their bubble or damage their faith: Jeremiah 29:11 does not apply to you or me right now. In fact, it didn't even apply to its original hearers.

Chapter 29 is a letter that Jeremiah writes from Jerusalem to a large group of Israelites who are being carried into exile by the Babylonians, and it is not a promise that God will rescue them. Through Jeremiah, God tells them that when they get there, they should unpack because they won't be going anywhere for a while. They should take wives, have kids, get jobs. They should pray for good things for the city because, for the foreseeable future, it will be their home.

Before He makes the 29:11 promise, God says that they will be there for 70 years before He will return to them. After all those old enough to read the letter will be dead.

In verse 11, God does promise that He has plans for the Jewish people in exile. Plans to give their people a bright future. Plans not to harm them but to give them a future filled with hope. To bless them that they might bless all nations. To reveal Himself to them that, through them, He might be revealed to the whole world. But not these exiles. They will die in Babylon.

Not exactly a compelling t-shirt slogan. Definitely not something that you'd hear on Christian TV. I was talking about this recently to someone who was shocked and disturbed at the possibility that I could be right. When I asked why, she said that it forced her to wrestle with what she had been teaching kids as memory verses and life lessons at camps. It jarred her because it made her question what she had believed and shared for years.

But then I asked her how she felt about Jeremiah 29:11 in the aftermath of her sexual assault. Her answer was that this verse was why it had taken so long to learn to trust God again and why it was still difficult.

As a teenager, she had been told constantly about God's plan, about this verse, about how Christianity ensured blessing and the hope of a bright future. When she was assaulted, however, her faith in this verse led her to one of two conclusions: either God did not keep His promises, or being attacked was part of God's bright future for her. In either scenario, it would be almost impossible to give herself to God fully again because it no longer came with guarantees. To affirm that God was good and that Jeremiah 29:11 applied to her meant that she had to either embrace her sexual assault or God's promise-breaking. Not only that, but she would have to affirm one of them as good.

The sermons we preach about God's provision are destructive when they lead us to paradoxical conclusions about the character of God and our experience of life.

But they're easy to preach because they make people feel comfortable, hopeful and generous to our ministry. Living in the parts of the world with health care and wealth means that these paradoxes are rarely exposed. We are not promised health or wealth or heaven now. But we are promised hardship and conflict, confusion and messiness. Heaven is sweet relief to those in exile, not to those who use their abundance to build their own personal paradise here.

Two Questions

In Luke 7, John the Baptist's public ministry has been brought to a halt and he is trapped in Herod's prison. Scared and alone, things are not looking good for him, so he sends his disciples to Jesus to ask him a question: 'Are you the one who was to come or should we expect someone else?'

As so often happens with rabbis in conversation and debate, there is a question within a question. Their conversation is layered. The immediately obvious question is 'Are you the Messiah, the one who was to come?'

Jesus answers the question, not with a yes or no, but with the promised actions of the Messiah in Isaiah 34 and 61: The blind see. The lame walk. The sick are cured. The deaf hear. The dead are raised. The Good News is preached to the poor. These are the signs that Israel has known to look out for when the Messiah comes, the supernatural actions of the One who will be their rescuer. But then Jesus ends

His response in a strange way: 'Blessed is he who does not fall away on account of me.'

Why would anyone fall away or stumble in their faith in seeing these amazing things? Surely this would gather people rather than push them away?

That brings us to the second question that John is asking, and that's 'Are you my Messiah?'

Because there is another promise of what the Messiah will do, a promise that relates profoundly to John's situation. A promise that Jesus deliberately leaves out of his list of the things that he is doing amongst the people:

> 'He has sent me to bind up the brokenhearted,
> to proclaim freedom for the captives
> and release from darkness for the prisoners.'
>
> Isaiah 61:1

It's a tragic conversation and a tragic answer. John asks, 'Are you the Messiah?' and 'Are you my Messiah?' because he knows that Jesus being one doesn't necessarily mean that He will be the other. He knows that Jesus can be the Messiah of Israel and Saviour of the whole world, but that doesn't mean John won't die in prison.

When John receives his answer, he is faced with the hardest of tensions. For him, to affirm Jesus as Lord is to affirm his own death and abandonment. To call Jesus the hope of the world is to acknowledge that there is no hope for him in

Herod's prison. Though I assume he was a far better man than me, if he is anything like me at all, the miraculous world-changing work of Jesus in the world around him is cold comfort on death row. No wonder Jesus says, 'Blessed is the one who does not fall away on account of me.' How great the temptation must have been to fall away when your cousin, your best friend, your Saviour and Messiah leaves you rotting in jail. It must have taken everything John had not to tear down the posters of kittens, sunsets and Jeremiah 29:11 that surely adorned his prison cell.

"This Teaching is Difficult. How Can We Accept it?"

In John 6, Jesus confounds everyone, from the Jews who opposed Him to the disciples who followed Him, when He talks about being the Bread of Life, and that you can't have life in Him without eating His flesh and drinking His blood.

Having taken Communion for most of my life, understanding the teaching here isn't difficult for me, but those listening must have thought He was advocating cannibalism and volunteering for the menu. Not only is Jesus not being comforting or affirming here, He's going out of His way to confuse and provoke. And many leave as a result. He is weeding out those who are following Him for the wrong reasons, deliberately reducing His followers to those who want, as Morpheus would say, to 'see how deep the rabbit hole goes.' He is calling those who are prepared to wrestle with the tension, to sit in unknowing, to be perplexed and yet fascinated.

So He turns to the Twelve and asks 'Are you still here? Are you not going with the rest of them?'

And Peter responds, 'Where else would we go? Only you have the words of life.'

The small print of following Jesus is tough. It promises that you won't have all the answers. It promises that things will be hard. It promises that tragedies will happen. It promises confusion, bewilderment and frustration. It promises dark nights of the soul and dark days. But where else would we go? Only Jesus has the words of life.

Chapter Three

WHY?

Faith Like A Child

In Matthew 18, the disciples come to Jesus asking, 'Who is the greatest in the Kingdom of Heaven?' Our immediate assumption when someone mentions 'Heaven' is that they refer to the place we go to be with God after we die, but not so here. Particularly in Matthew's Gospel, but in the others as well, when Jesus refers to the Kingdom of Heaven, He's talking about the movement of His followers that are bringing the life and way of God to the Earth in the here and now.

This question has been a long time coming and, despite Jesus' rebukes, the disciples continue to obsess over which of them is the greatest (Mark 9 and Luke 9). They're still arguing about it at The Last Supper when they really should have other things on their minds.

When asked in Matthew's account, Jesus calls a child and has him stand in their midst and says, 'Unless you turn and become like children, you will never enter the Kingdom of Heaven. Whoever humbles himself like this child is the greatest in the Kingdom of Heaven.'

Trust Jesus to pull the rug out from under their feet and confound them. And us.

In a culture obsessed with growing up, 'becoming like a child' feels like going backwards. So much depends on what we consider childlikeness to mean. Because He's not talking about childishness.

It's especially difficult for me to make this argument because I don't particularly like children. There are a couple of exceptions (like my quasi-nephews) but, for the most part, children terrify me. They are an enigma, mainly because they don't play by the same rules as the rest of the world. And it is precisely for this reason that I think Jesus says we must be like them to enter into the Kingdom of Heaven. I'm no expert on children but what follows are some of my observations on how they live. From a distance, obviously, because children tend to be sticky.

Children don't seem to acknowledge the things that I think make me valuable. They don't care how well I can speak or write or how many people read my blog. I'm so conditioned to respond to situations based on what people want from me that I struggle to know how to be with them, or even who to be, because I don't know what kids want from me. The truth that they just want my presence reminds me that sometimes I don't know how to be present as myself (yes,

I am aware of what this says about me and I'm trying to work through it!).

Children trust. The other day I was playing with my best friend Matt's son Joshua, with whom, though it's taken a long time, I feel like I'm building a good relationship. I was messing with him and throwing him in the air when, stupidly, I threw him too high and hit his head off the ceiling. Though he was shocked and hurt, he didn't cry because it was me throwing him. I worked hard to keep laughing and pretend it was all part of the game. If I had panicked, he would have cried, but because I didn't freak out, neither did he. His trust is beautiful. He interprets the world around him through love and relationship rather than suspicion or competition.

Children are willing to experiment; they're not afraid of looking like failures. Joshua, who is four years old, can use an iPhone far better than my dad because he doesn't overthink it, he just immerses himself in what might and might not work. I love Mike Yaconelli's observation that if you ask a group of adults if they can draw or dance or sing, they'll answer based on what they consider proficiency in each area and whether or not they match up to the standard. But if you ask a group of children, most of them will shout 'Yes!' because they haven't yet been beaten down into believing that to dance or draw or sing, you need to be good at it.

Children seem to be more open. When they hear fantastical stories, they don't get lost in the details of historical accuracy, they get lost in the beauty of it. They're idealistic. They haven't turned themselves off to what might be possible. They truly believe that anything could happen.

Finally, they ask 'Why?' and they won't settle for the word 'because' as an answer. They want to know, they want to challenge, they want to understand. And when the answers they are given don't make sense or appear to be dodging the question, they aren't afraid to say it. And as long as they keep asking 'Why?', they will always be growing and changing, something that we as adults sometimes forget to keep doing.

Working with Teens

If the human life is like clay on a wheel in motion being shaped by the hands of many potters, then children scare me because their clay is still so fluid and unpredictable. Every bit of pressure makes an impact, but once made, it can often be smoothed out easily. Adults and older people scare me because, without a conscious effort to resist it, the older people get, the drier and more brittle they tend to become. For many, change does not shape them, it breaks them.

Teenagers, however, are that bizarre middle ground that makes youth work so fascinating, exhilarating and rewarding. They are still technically children, but with greater ability to reason and communicate. They are taking shape but the outcome is not certain. They are open, curious and dynamic while also being capable of grappling with the world around them philosophically and theologically. There are many things that you can say about God or life to adults without being challenged, but teenagers won't let you off the hook so easily. They ask fantastic questions, some of which we can answer, some we have never considered, and some that we are too scared to ask.

While some adults hear the 'rules' or commandments of Christianity and start trying to obey them, teenagers will often refuse to until they understand why.

One might ask about the virtues of such an attitude, and to many it may seem arrogant or rebellious, but if we dig a little deeper and ask why they think this way, we actually find a beautiful approach to life.

Firstly, teenagers are very conscious that they have one life to live and want to get the most out of it. If they perceive in a rule or guideline something that will limit their experience of life, they are not prepared to obey it for the sake of obedience. There is nothing more off-putting to a teenager than going through the motions or living primarily out of obligation, especially when it comes to rules.

Secondly, they are still deciding whether or not they can trust God. Asking 'Why?' is their way of trying to figure out the heart of God and what He says about life. If they find wisdom and beauty behind the rule or if it reveals a compelling way of living, they will often obey it with a passion that adults cannot muster.

Finally, they don't want to be sheep. They don't want to simply inherit their faith and lifestyle, they want to own it. In the same way that they are starting to make decisions about their future, their career, their relationships, they want the opportunity to explore their faith and see whether or not it is something they want in their own lives. It's like trying on a piece of clothing before buying it: they want to see how it fits, how it looks and how it feels.

So they ask 'Why?'--not because they want to be rebellious, not because they want to annoy us, but because they legitimately want to know. The tragedy is that many of us are caught off guard by this because we've never actually asked 'Why?' ourselves.

Christian Questions

The questions of children and teens should not just be tolerated, they should be celebrated. Pete Rollins points out that a key difference between Judaism and Islam is in their names. Islam means 'to submit,' so obedience becomes a core value in the faith of Muslims figuring out how to live in the way that they believe Allah has called them to. Jews and Christians, however, take their identity from God's renaming of Jacob. Jacob's name means 'he supplants' which is to take away someone's else's place, usually in an underhanded way. God changes his name to 'wrestled with God' after Jacob wrestles with a messenger from God and won't let him go until he blesses him. The name is part of the blessing, as is the limp that he carries forever after he has his hip put out of socket, and both are part of the stories of his descendants. They constantly wrestle with God, getting it right and getting it wrong, being cast out into exile and being brought home to rebuild.

Wrestling with God and what it means to follow Him is hardwired into the Judeo-Christian tradition. When God gives the Law to Moses and the people of Israel, they soon discover that it is deliberately complex and, at times, even paradoxical. There are situations where one must choose what law to obey and what to break because they come into conflict. Arguments and heated conversations kick off about how to follow God because it's not as simple as just obeying, it has to be interpreted and weighed; decisions must be made. And this constant tension brings growth. The friction brings wisdom, philosophy and humility.

The Rabbinical teaching tradition develops, and they begin to use questions as a way of conversing, learning and teaching. Debates were won when a Rabbi posed a question that the other couldn't answer without contradicting their original argument. Questions and wrestling birthed Rabbinical wisdom and, at the best of times, kept the nation of Israel learning and growing in their understanding of God.

So it's no surprise that when Joseph and Mary return to Jerusalem to find Jesus (after leaving without him!) that they find the twelve-year-old Messiah in the Temple 'sitting around the teachers, listening to them and asking them questions' (Luke 2:46). This passage can conjure an image of a meek and mild, milk-bottle Jesus gazing adoringly at the teachers filling Him with knowledge in response to His questions, but that's not the picture Luke is painting.

Jesus is both asking questions and responding to the teachers, and people are amazed by His understanding. He is not demonstrating Himself to be a genius at Bible-themed table quizzes or 'sword drills,' He is challenging the religious leaders, confounding them and catching them out. Even His response to His parents' disciplining is a question that they can't answer without looking fools! I can't help think that the pre-teen Jesus who amazed first-century rabbis would have been kicked out of Sunday School if He went to church these days.

Asking Why?

Asking 'Why?' is not just a mark of adolescence and child-like faith, it's also become a hallmark of the 21st century and what some call post-modern culture. It's not just our teenagers asking 'Why?'--it's our whole culture, and many Christians and churches are suddenly finding themselves ill-equipped to respond at the end of modernity where the primary questions were 'What?' and 'How?'

For example, for two hundred years, a debate has been raging within the church and between the church and culture about how the world was created. The prevailing opinion outside the church is that the world was created in the aftermath of the 'Big Bang' and that humans came into existence by evolution as life developed on our planet. Many churches (though not as many as in the past) argue that God created the world in six days according to Genesis, that humans were made in the image of God and the world is somewhere between four and six thousand years old. For a long time, the question has been 'How was the world created?' and the winner of this argument would be seen to be the one who 'held the truth'.

At the end of the 20th and beginning of the 21st century, Scot McKnight points out that a different question is being asked. That question is, 'If God created the world in six days, why did He make it look like it evolved?' It's not a question of methodology any more, it's a question about the heart of God. Can He truly be good if He made the world one way and yet made it look like something else? If that's the case, does that not mean that God deliberately puts a stumbling block in the way of people believing? What sort of God would do that? A good God? This concerns postmoderns far more than how the world was created. Strangely enough, they might be able to embrace the argument for God's creation and at the same time refuse His embrace because they can't trust Him.

The issue of faith today is no longer one of scientific truth, it is one of beauty, love and goodness. During modernity, many Christians dissected the Bible to find the scientific and historical evidence for its veracity but didn't realise that, like J.M. Synge's definition of a critic, they were slitting the throat of 'a skylark to see what makes it sing'. It's like scratching the paint off the Mona Lisa to see if Da Vinci left a date on the canvas. You may find the answer to the question you're asking but lose what the artist was trying to communicate. If we are to have 'faith like children,' we must approach the Bible differently, no longer counting the bones to see if we have the numbers right but searching for truth that changes us in the blood and guts: the tension and the challenge of the Story itself.

Back to the Crime Scene

One could easily liken the last three hundred years to a courtroom drama. The Church as God's defence attorney, the atheistic community as the prosecution, our culture and society as the jury weighing up the arguments of the evidence presented to it. It's adversarial, argumentative and often just plain nasty. Both sides present their cases with life-or-death passion because their identity and survival rest on the verdict. Honesty and humility are not virtues in this arena. It's not just about being right, it's about everyone seeing that you're right. But to enter the courtroom, one must leave the crime scene, the place of discovery. The investigation must end for the trial to begin.

The best metaphor I can think of for the time in which we live is that the modernist trial of Christianity has resulted in a hung jury. We are no longer lawyers defending God's case, we are detectives returning to the scene of the crime. Something has happened––that much is clear––and it's the reason that we are all here.

So we stand shoulder-to-shoulder with other detectives with different perspectives, searching for the fingerprints of the One who made everything happen. To enter the Kingdom of God, we must abandon our tendency to be lawyers, lobbyists and marketers whose lifestyle and identity rests on a particular verdict. We must be detectives, archaeologists and explorers. Not adults looking to be proven right but children searching for what is right. Looking for evidence. For motive. For truth.

Chapter Four

A SECOND LOOK

The temptation can be to approach the Bible dispassionately and at a distance, scouring the text for statements of truth for us to live by. The problem is this serves only to let us know about God, not to actually know him. One of the things that I tell my students who are interested in reading the Bible is to read it imaginatively. To encounter Him, we must go beyond reading the text to reading ourselves into the text, imagining ourselves in the shoes or sandals of characters within the story, especially those who encounter Jesus and sometimes even Jesus himself. Approaching the text like this can often bring us to different, deeper conclusions, offering hope and inspiration to those who are trying to figure out how to be Christians in the 21st century.

The Dead Girl and the Sick Woman

Many of us would say that we all need to encounter Jesus but, if we're honest, it's what scares us most. What would

He say? What would He point to in our lives that needs to change? How would His face look when He looked at me? What would I see in His eyes? And it's not just a 21st-century feeling.

In Luke 8, Jesus is called on by Jairus, a ruler of the synagogue, who begs Jesus to come to his house and heal his daughter. As Jesus and His disciples make their way to the house, a crowd is pressing in on them, no doubt shouting questions and requests for the miracle worker that everyone wants a piece of.

Making no noise, however, is a woman in the crowd who has had a bleeding disorder for 12 years. She is making her way toward Jesus in spite of the people milling around Him. She is silent, unknown and taking a massive risk. Her condition excludes her from the Temple as she is not only ceremonially unclean, but unclean to the touch. By being in this crowd, she makes everyone she touches unclean and, if discovered, the penalty would be severe, possibly even death. She may pay for it with her life.

In our world, it's hard to imagine her pain and shame. She cannot touch her husband, her family, her friends. She can't shake someone's hand or pass them a tea towel without making them dirty and removing them from the presence of God. Though there is no direct equivalent in our time, the feeling is not uncommon. So many of the teens and adults I work with feel this perpetual sense of shame, a conviction that they are dirty to the touch, unworthy and unfit to be in the presence of the divine.

Finally she gets within touching distance and reaches out to grab His tzit-tzit, the corner of His cloak from which His prayer tassel hangs. By taking hold of the corner of His garment, she is also taking hold of promises spoken long ago, for the tassel is the corner, the Hebrew word for which also means 'wing' and, when the Messiah comes, He will 'arise with healing in his wings' (Malachi 4:2). It is a declaration of faith, a proclamation of His identity, a reaching for hope, both brave and cowardly at the same time. [2]

She is brave in that she risks death in pursuing the One who can rescue her, putting her faith and life under the 'wings' of the One who was to come. In doing so, she gets what she wants––but not what she needs.

She is cowardly in that she wants the easy way, the salvation without the encounter. She follows a religious formula to find the location of healing but runs in fear from the Messiah turning and acknowledging her in her brokenness and uncleanness.

Fully healed, she turns and begins to make her way out of the crowd before she is discovered. I can only imagine how her blood must have run cold when Jesus asks 'Who touched

[2] The work of Rob Bell and David Stern's Jewish New Testament Commentary have been crucial to my understanding and interpretation of this passage.

me?' I imagine her frozen, eyes closed tightly, gritting her teeth and hoping desperately that He is talking about someone else. Suddenly, there is no way out. She knows He knows. I love the descriptions of her turning to Him.

'Seeing that she could not go unnoticed.' *NIV*

'When she saw that she was not hidden.' *NRSV*

After 12 years on the outside, of being unclean to the touch, of being contagious and ashamed, she can no longer remain unnoticed. She can no longer be hidden, whether by the desires of others or her own. She came seeking healing but Jesus gives her wholeness. She sought respite from her sickness but finds restoration in her community and in her own eyes.

So she turns and falls trembling before Him and tells her story.

And Jesus responds, 'Daughter, your faith has made you well. Go in peace.'

Her faith formula brings her healing, but it is her encounter that brings her peace.

So much of my Christian life has taught me to be this woman. To go to Jesus for what I want. So I pray for healing, for opportunity, for help. I want all these different things and I approach Jesus for them. But, whether the prayer is answered or not, I try and sneak away before He can notice me, look at me, meet me. I have spent so much of my Christian life trying to master the formula of getting what I want without having to have the encounter that I fear. I seek the solution or resolution but leave before I get the peace, I take the healing but refuse the wholeness. I go to Jesus for what I want without trusting Him to give me what I need.

A second look at the story does not give us a formula for tugging on the robes of Jesus, it exposes our tendency to embrace formulaic Christianity. What initially looks like courage and devotion exposes our fear of encounter and our lack of trust. A second look at her story challenges us to take a second look at ourselves and how we allow our fear and shame to dictate what God can and can't do in our lives.

"Doubting" Thomas

For almost 2,000 years, Thomas the disciple has had to live with an adverb attached to his name that paints him in a bad light and calls into question his faith and devotion to Jesus. If those who have died can indeed look down upon those who are living, I wonder how frustrating it must be for him to be distinguished from all other Thomases as the one who doubted. I don't think he would be frustrated for being judged and found wanting, but for being misunderstood and watching us miss the point. At first glance, Thomas's refusal to believe that Jesus has risen from the dead looks like a character flaw or failure … but only until it's juxtaposed against the alternative.

At the end of John 19, Jesus is dead and buried. The miracle worker, the preacher, the leader, the Messiah: dead. It's a dark day for everyone, but particularly for those who were closest to Him. Spectators lost a public Jesus, the one who had taught them, healed them and brought hope to them. Those who followed Jesus, both men and women, lost the one who called them, rescued them, challenged and changed them. They lost a brother, a father, a confidant and friend. Their purpose, identity and hope died with him. At least until He shook off death's chains and came back, changing everything. It's one of those moments in history that I think every Christian would give anything to have witnessed.

It's easy for us as 21st-century Christians to judge the disciples for not seeing it coming or believing that it would happen, especially when we read His predictions just a couple of chapters before His death. But we weren't there for the final dinner, we weren't with Him in the garden. We didn't watch the nails pierce Him or watch Him breathe His last. We didn't see the sky go dark and feel that darkness cast a shadow over our hearts and hopes. We understand its necessity, we know the whole story. For us, it's already resolved and fixed. We don't have the tension of the time between His death and rising. We can't imagine what it would have been like to be there in the midst of it, trying to recall the words of Jesus in our minds over the weeping of our hearts or the deafening silence as we sit together, unable to find any words that would bring even the possibility of hope.

Mary Magdalene goes to the tomb to grieve and finds it empty. She calls on Peter and John to come see; they too see that it's empty. Even then, they don't know what's happened. The possibility of resurrection, no matter how many times Jesus told them about it, doesn't even enter their minds. It's impossible. It's too good to be true. It's too much to believe. So Peter and John go back to their houses and miss seeing Jesus appear to Mary Magdalene. They don't see Jesus until He walks through a locked door and stands in their midst. They are amazed, moved, restored. But Thomas was not there. And when they come to him and tell him of what they have seen, he says:

> 'Unless I put my finger in the mark of the nails and my hand in his side, I will not believe.'

Poor 'doubting' Thomas. Why didn't he believe? Why couldn't he muster enough faith to proclaim that Jesus had risen?

Perhaps because belief is not the central issue of Thomas's story. Perhaps it's because whether or not Thomas believed in Jesus was not as important as how much he loved Him.

The closest I can get to putting on Thomas' shoes and walking through his experience is to imagine my father dying. My dad means more to me than words can say. Some say that they struggle to engage with God as Father because of their family experience. That has not been my story. My hope is that I discover God to be as good as my father is.

So if he passed from this world and my family came to me a few days later and said they had seen him alive, I would not believe them. Not until I saw it. Because it's not about belief. It's about humanity and love. If my father's light were to be extinguished then, for a long time, so would mine. It would crush me and I don't know how I would recover.

What would your reaction be if you saw my family come to me and say that my father was alive again and I said, 'Wow, that's cool'?

A little bit anti-climactic isn't it? You'd have to question whether or not I cared.

What if Thomas had said, 'Great! I'm so glad Jesus is alive!'? It would be faith… but it wouldn't necessarily be love.

Thomas's response is beautiful because it denies truth in favour of love for the sake of his heart. Watching Jesus die was the most painful thing he had ever experienced. His world changed when Jesus died. It ended. So he can't affirm Jesus' life after death because his life is intertwined with Jesus'. When Jesus died, so did he. And he is not prepared to hope again, to love again, to live again unless he knows it's real.

Thomas did not have too little faith to believe. He had too much love for belief to be taken lightly.

A second look at the story challenges us not to ask whether or not we believe but whether or not we love. Whether or not our lives are entwined with the life of Jesus. It exposes how we reward intellectual affirmation of orthodoxy without addressing our lack of devotion and love. Belief is cheap; love is expensive. Belief can happen without love; love can make belief difficult. Belief asks us to take an intellectual stand on one side or another; love requires us to actually stand there.

Judas: Unswerving Obedience to his own Personal Jesus

While some may be able to live with taking a second look at the story of 'Doubting Thomas', most are loathe to learn lessons from the life of Judas. While Thomas's name received an unpleasant addition, Judas' name has become synonymous with his story, an insult reserved for those who do not honour bonds of friendship, those who sell out the people closest to them, those who would hurt anyone to make a quick buck.

While it's clear from the Gospels that Judas sold Jesus out to the Pharisees, what isn't clear is why. What was he hoping would happen? And did he get what he hoped for? Before the Last Supper, Judas goes and meets with the Pharisees and agrees on a price to betray him: thirty pieces of silver. Just a month's wages to give up the One he had followed for three years, the One who had forgiven him after he was caught taking money from their community funds. A small price for a high prize. It's a strange move from a man who was outraged at a woman who spent a year's wages worth of perfume washing Jesus' feet in an outrageous act of worship.

I wonder if there is method in his madness. If the price is actually a stroke of genius. Low enough to be affordable, high enough to be convincing. I wonder if Judas was living according to the myth of the military Messiah, the One who would defeat the corrupt Jewish leadership and overthrow the occupation of the Roman Empire. If so, then he would be looking for an excuse to sell Jesus out. It's part of a plan, not to see Him defeated, but to see Him triumphant.[3]

The more that I have been thinking about this, the more I have wondered what it would have been like to be Judas. Believing that your betrayal was actually the ultimate in loyalty if it would force Jesus' hand and cause Him to reveal Himself to the world. What it would be like to take the money with a smile and think, 'You don't even realise that you have just bought your own destruction! I can't wait to see you try and take Him down!'

I wonder if Judas would have felt something like this if he had lived long enough to see the crucifixion.

[3] A big thanks to Pete Rollins and Bishop Michael Burrows, two thinkers who have dramatically challenged my understanding of Judas.

I am Judas, believing that my betrayal would be his revelation.

Believing hands on him would be flung off. That if the conflict came he would rise up, not go down.

I am Judas and I wanted him to be revealed, not reviled, followed, not flogged, the victor, not the victim.

I am Judas casting pieces of silver at priests and leaders I thought would be cast aside.

I am Judas weeping as the one who spoke us into existence has death spoken over him.

I am Judas crying 'Come down!' as those around me turn it into a taunt.

I am Judas watching the one who healed, scarred, the one who fed, starved, the who loved, hated, the who forgave, condemned.

I am Judas holding my breath as he breathes out and darkness breaks in.

I am Judas suspended in the air by guilt and shame entwined into a noose that holds me aloft until my kicking stops.

I am Judas afraid that this is the end.

I am Judas afraid that it is not.

I am Judas wondering if when he said 'Forgive them for they know not what they do …" if he meant me.

I think Judas truly loved Jesus, partially for who He was, partially for what Judas believed He had come to do. He believed that Jesus had come to bring freedom. And He did--but not from the Roman Empire or Herod as Judas supposed.

The Rhinoceros Renaissance

There's a great cartoon that someone posted on Reddit a while ago that showed a Rhino painting landscapes on an easel. The landscape looks beautiful but every painting is spoiled by the Rhino's horn in the middle of each canvas. He can't see the world without seeing something of himself in it. It's the same with Judas--and most of us. He can't look at Jesus without placing on Him his own desires and longings. No matter how many times he hears Jesus say that He is going to die and be raised from the dead, Judas finds a way to ignore it in order to keep his own dreams alive. It's probably not even a conscious decision, he just can't see past his own horn.

The traditional interpretation of this passage is appealing because it is so specific that it's almost irrelevant to our daily lives. But if the root of his failure is basing his life and decisions on a mental picture of Jesus defined by his own agenda rather than who Jesus claims to be, then a lot more of us are guilty of it than we might first think. One of the biggest dangers that we face in the 21st century is the temptation to follow Jesus because of what Christian marketers have promised us, rather than in response to Jesus Himself. It's what Jesus is talking about in Matthew 11 when He says:

> *But to what will I compare this generation?*
> *It is like children sitting in the market-places*
> *and calling to one another,*
> *"We played the flute for you and you did not dance;*
> *We wailed and you did not mourn"*

Matthew 11:17

You are upset because you played a happy song and I didn't dance. You complain because you sing a sad song and I did not cry. You're angry because you painted a picture of me and I look nothing like it.

Chapter Five

OF TWO SONS

Some say that a picture is worth a thousand words. Dan Pink argues that a good metaphor is worth a thousand pictures.[4] And that's exactly what many Christians think parables are: metaphors that Jesus gave to make faith simpler.

But a parable is far more than a metaphor. Metaphors break down and are generally used to communicate a single truth or answer a particular question. Parables, however, break us down. They are designed to expose our brokenness and bias. They don't simplify, they complicate. Their purpose is not to show people what side to take on an issue but to show them how their perception has been blind-sided by their own issues. Parables are not answers, they are deeper and better questions.

Like the story of the woman at the well, the Parable of the Lost Son is a passage that is destroyed when it is oversimplified

---

[4] From the video version of his book, A Whole New Mind, which can be found on YouTube.

as a metaphor. Jesus tells the story in response to the Pharisees and the scribes who are grumbling amongst themselves when they realise that tax collectors and sinners are coming to Jesus to hear his teaching. Many of us grew up with a watered down version of this story that spoke of prodigal sons who should come home with their tails between their legs and older brothers who should be more gracious when they do. The younger son is the villain, the father is the hero and the older brother learns the moral of the story.

The metaphor of the Prodigal Son perpetuates a life of labelling, boxing and judging people. When we oversimplify the story, all Jesus is doing is challenging their grumbling and calling for more grace, but we miss the point that Jesus is really making: that there are two ways of running from God, two ways of losing ourselves and losing Him, the foreign land and the field. Jesus is not telling a story about a right place and a wrong place, He is giving us a spectrum upon which we all find ourselves in the mess we make of trying to follow Jesus. He is not telling a story of insiders and outsiders, of right people and wrong people, but is revealing to them and to us the complexity of the Christian journey. That we are not where we think we are.

Simple Labels for Complex Places

I have often heard the Christian journey defined in terms that make it difficult for me to figure out where I am on the spectrum. There are new Christians (not me, I've been a 'Christian' for pretty much my whole life), backsliding Christians (it's not uncommon for me to take two steps forward and one backward, and vice versa), nominal Christians (sometimes I feel like my faith permeates everything in my life, at other times I feel like it affects nothing) and mature Christians (how do I define maturity? Is it my lifestyle or my thoughts? Conscious thoughts or unconscious attitudes?). Some Christians talk about the journey like it's a staircase on which their current position can be clearly plotted, but for me it feels more like a game of snakes and ladders. Sometimes what I believe shapes how I feel, and I live directly out of it. Sometimes I can't feel it but still try to live out what I believe. Sometimes I live in direct opposition to what I believe. Sometimes I'm climbing ladders and journeying up hills at pace. Sometimes I feel like I'm free-falling, hurtling past sights I saw on the way up, back towards where I began. Sometimes I'm afraid I'm going to fall off the board altogether.

I am none of these terms completely, and yet all of them partially. I am constantly re-discovering my faith and the heart of God and starting over, constantly succeeding and failing, living nominally and living passionately with nothing but a night's sleep in between. Sometimes I'm flirting with maturity, sometimes embracing childishness. My journey is shades of grey, the lines blurred, blending my light and my darkness making it hard to distinguish in any moment or action where one begins and the other ends.

Being Both Sons

If my experience of growing up in church is anything to go by, I imagine it would be a difficult thing growing up in God's house like the sons in the story. Many of us found ourselves learning about God before we began a journey of actually knowing Him. Something that messed with me was the disparity between what was taught and what was implied.

I was told that God celebrated my creativity and exuberance--but I was supposed to be quiet during the service. I was told that God accepted me just as I am--but I needed to dress smart to come to church. I was taught that God forgave all my sins--but His followers seemed to have the memory of a herd of elephants.

The choices of both sons in the story are based on misunderstandings of the Father's heart, and I'd wager it's not because of what they learnt about Him from their experiences with Him but how their--and our-- insecurities can define what we learn as we interpret the world around us.

The younger son has come to believe that life cannot be found at home. We often put this down to the rebelliousness of youth, foolishness, or the absence of a moral compass; that's a convenient conclusion, especially if the reason the younger son left is because he doesn't want to become like his brother. As distasteful and challenging as that may be, it fits well with the challenge that Jesus is bringing, that the Pharisees who look down on the 'tax collectors and sinners' are not just devoid of solution, they are also part of the problem.

Either way, the younger son believes that there is more to the world, that life is found in what he can taste, feel and touch. So he takes his inheritance, his heritage, his identity and he goes out and spends it, he spends himself, on every experience that he can find. He falls, like so many of us, for the lie that wealth, sex and substances can bring life. As a friend in college used to joke, he spends everything he has, and is, on fast women and slow horses. In his attempt to find life, he loses it. He gains the world, loses it and loses his soul in the process.

When I hit my teenage years, I was the younger son. I knew all about the father, knew His house inside out, saw the obedient 'older brothers' all around me and wanted neither their faith nor their lives. As I looked on, they seemed bound to their duty, to colouring within the lines and ticking all the right boxes. I was disturbed to see what felt like the presence of my school principal invade my weekend. Rules. Duty. Work. Obligation. Good behaviour. It didn't inspire passion or engagement when I was too young to make choices about attendance, so I sought life elsewhere.

I had my first drink and cigarette when I was 12, a triple shot of vodka in my friend John's bathroom… and it was incredible. It was exhilarating, exciting, edgy and dangerous. I felt alive, like I was truly experiencing what life could be and I couldn't get enough of it. Christians were so wrong about alcohol: it wasn't evil or dirty, it was amazing, it offered escape, rebellion, the feeling of finally making my own decisions... and girls! I was loving it and loving life. I began to live for the weekend, and the thought of a weekend without a party or drink was unthinkable.

I'd love to break into 'testimony' mode and be able to say that I saw a light, realised that I was wrong and ruining my life, or that my life spun out of control... but it didn't. I was having the time of my life, even if I didn't like the hiding, the lying or showing up to church hungover. I was loving youth group with Christians on Monday night and loving alcohol on the weekends and that was fine.

But eventually, you come to a point where the excitement wears off and what initially was thrilling becomes mundane and routine. Still, you keep going because you lack the imagination or desire to find other ways to stave off the boredom, especially when you're growing up in Bangladesh where there isn't exactly a lot to do by Western standards.

When I got back to Ireland, I thought everything would change, that life would be packed with all the things I missed in Dhaka, but I fell back into the same patterns: searching for fulfillment, enjoyment, excitement and life at the bottom of a bottle, the end of a joint or the lips of a beautiful girl.

Soon after returning home, I started attending Christian camps because it sounded like a great way to meet friends (girls in particular) and experienced God both inadvertently and accidentally. I was suddenly confronted with a God who could be known rather than just known about, a God who could be experienced. I went up for every altar call, to get saved, to speak in tongues, to get pushed over, to grow underarm hair. Whatever was on offer, I was there. This was a faith that I could believe in and live for, and I became a strange hybrid of the older and younger son, finding life on the lips of the preacher during the services and life on the lips of a pretty girl behind the sports hall when the service ended.

I was the younger son because I still believed that life could be found in living on the edge, in breaking the rules, in drinking in the experiences of rebellion. But when my inheritance was spent and I found myself in the pigsty, I would pack up and move what little I had back home: to church, to camp, to Christ.

Somehow, though, I bypassed the Father on the way home. I must have snuck past Him in the night, forsaking the ring and the sandals, the robe and the party, and stolen into the field alongside my older brother where I would pick up my tools and set myself to work, building up enough wealth to return to a land far away with the wages that I earned. My economy operated on grace vouchers that can be easily redeemed on Friday and Saturday night, only to be recharged or replaced on Sunday mornings.

The life of the older son seems completely opposite on the outside, but is a reaction to a misunderstanding of the Father nonetheless. This son grows up with responsibility, joining his Father in the fields from an early age, the life of the home and the life of the field dangerously intertwined. For him to be a son is to be in the fields, his identity, purpose and place all dependent on the field rather than at the fireplace where parent and child share life.

There's no surprise, then, at his reaction to his disobedient brother returning home. His life is so focused on the fields that it is only after the party is in full swing that he approaches the house to hear what's happened. Long after the Father has returned home to wait for his youngest, long after the servants have left the fields and started setting up the celebration, he returns home exhausted, probably forced by failing light and tasks he cannot achieve alone. Drained from his obedience, self-righteous because of his undying loyalty, he is filled with rage and hurt at the very idea of a banquet for this son they should have disowned rather than rescued. And his question tells us everything: "For him you slaughter the fattened calf and I don't even get a goat to party with my friends? Where is my celebration? Do my years of service not mean that I deserve it? Have I not earned your love?"

Those words roll off my tongue so easily, never spoken (my silence in the name of being gracious), but so present in my heart since I started taking seriously what it means to follow God.

It's not that I resent those who come home--I love it when they do and try to live my life fighting to bring them home. And yet the freshness of their received grace makes me ache when mine has become stale. So often I have seen my Christian life driven by a need to earn love, to be celebrated for my undying loyalty and my exhaustion from giving my life for Jesus. So often I live like God's love, affection and acceptance can be earned from the number of people I have preached to, the amount of 'lost reached' and the quantity of tears shed--but I find it doesn't change how God sees me, my position before Him or, more often, my position in relation to everyone else before Him. The field is also a foreign land, a place of stages, pulpits and microphones that I believe will give me the life that everything else failed to bestow.

I am two sons.

I seek life in wildness, excitement and rebellion, in everything that shimmers and shines.

I seek life in things that will provide temporary escape but ultimately destroy it completely.

I come home to work, rather than to live.

I spend too much of myself in His fields and too little at His feet.

I mistakenly believe that I--and perhaps we--need to earn what I already have, robbing God of what He truly wants but will not forcefully take: my presence, my heart.

A Third Son

During a sermon I preached in Bible College, it didn't go down particularly well when I placed Jesus in a creative re-imagining of this story. But I'm not sure we can fully understand the parable without Jesus' presence in it.

I imagine him as a third son, the eldest, who not only truly understands the Father but understands his brothers. The picture in my head is of the Father and His Son sitting at the fire in silence, heartbroken by the absence of their family. They mourn the loss of the youngest, miles away, going from party to party and bed to bed, looking for life and always waking up empty. They fear for his physical safety and for the destruction and desolation of his heart as he pursues everything that promises life but instead consumes and destroys him.

Their hearts ache for the elder of the sons, a matter of yards away physically but emotionally as far as his younger brother, as he works past dusk trying to earn the place that has been set for him and that he has left vacant.

Unable to passively watch, they concoct a plan that only a mad God could come up with, for the eldest son to pursue his brothers and loose the chains that bind them to every place other than home.

He finds one in a foreign land, the other in a field, and fights to convince both to come home.

Apparently I took the parable too far, taking liberties with the passage, but I'm not so sure. Every word, story and action of Jesus is a keyhole through which we can glimpse as much as we can take of the heart of the Father and begin to understand more fully, though never completely, the mystery of His death and resurrection, the mystery of a God who could not stand back and do nothing.

I think, for many of us, it's not as simple as being one son or the other. I feel as though I live on both sides of the house. Wearied by my experience of the field, I journey to foreign lands. Wearied by my experience of foreign lands, I journey past the house, straight out to the fields, trying to earn things that are already mine. I attend every party and yet never attend the party. I work for the Father but am never truly with Him.

For me, the hardest part of the Christian life is to be at home. To believe the unbelievable: that I belong with and to God, that He not only loves me but also likes me, that He doesn't want me for what I can do but for who I am. To be still and know. To find life in the place I never expected. To abandon foreign lands and fields to find life at His feet. To believe and live into what is too good to be true and is yet the only truth that will save me, the only life in which I can be truly free.

Chapter Six

HOME

'If we were created in God's image then when
God was a child he smushed fire ants with his
fingertips and avoided tough questions.'

- Buddy Wakefield

The biggest battle of my Christian life has been feeling at
home with God. Intimacy with God was a foreign concept
to me, reserved for saints, politicians and televangelists.
For me growing up, God always felt like the old man in the
sky with a stick. Unmerciful, unflinching, unsmiling, He
looked down on the world--and me in particular--without
emotion or fondness, his eyes unreadable and uncertain.
Prayer felt to me like sitting outside the principal's office
when I was in school, trying to figure out how to get away
with my wrongdoing, and church felt like being at a fancy
dinner and not knowing which fork to use.

So much of my work with young people has been focused
on understanding the character of God because it has been
so hard for me to see Him as more than angry, petty and

rules-obsessed. It was as if He stood in Heaven, parted the clouds and watched my life without any discernible interest, ready to strike when I stepped out of line or broke one of His ridiculous rules. It was only then that a smile would flicker across His face as He got the justification He needed to lash out and punish me, like the God in Gary Larson's brilliant Far Side cartoon, watching human life on a computer monitor, His finger hovering over the 'SMITE' button. This G/god didn't exactly provoke desires within me to pray, pursue holiness or sing songs about how amazing He is. I feared Him, and––to be brutally honest––I hated Him for it. I decided just to put my head down, colour within the lines and hold out for Heaven where I would finally be transformed into the sort of person that could satisfy His unreasonable and unachievable standards.

Sunday School Simplicity

Sunday School has a lot to answer for. I know that Sunday School teachers have the best of intentions, but I wonder if we are told stories as children that we have no business hearing until we have the intellectual capacity to hear them.

The presence of animals and rainbows in the story of Noah and his ark doesn't make it philosophically palatable. By the time we are teenagers we are no longer entertained by the flannel animals and have become suspicious of a God who considers genocide a solution to any problem. The fun we had dancing and shouting around an imaginary

Jericho kept my attention deficit disorder under control as a kid. But as a teen it was cold comfort when I saw pictures of families trapped under rubble from earthquakes and tsunamis and wondered if that was what the fall of Jericho was like.

I've always struggled with the story of Abraham being called to sacrifice Isaac. Abraham responds to God's call and leaves his home and people for an unknown land. He believes that God will fulfil His promise to give him descendents despite his age. And he isn't getting any younger. Sarah laughs at God's promise, but Abraham believes. He follows God for 25 years, often wandering, often facing struggle, seeing Sodom and Gomorrah destroyed, seemingly no closer to the land God is bringing him to. And then, after a quarter of a century, he finally has his promised son and God asks him to climb a mountain in Moriah and offer this promised child as a sacrifice.

I could make more sense of this request if it had happened at the beginning of the story, if it was a test to show whether or not Abraham was to be trusted. But he has already given everything--yet God asks for what he has left. Despite all his sacrifices, God asks him to give up the result and reward of his patience and faithfulness. It just doesn't sit right. Why this? Even though God never intended for Abraham to sacrifice Isaac, why put him through this after everything else he has survived and suffered through?

Even though it ends well, it can leave a nasty aftertaste for those of us who become familiar with it at a young age. A sly and subtle belief takes root in the dark recesses of our mind. Like Shylock in *The Merchant of Venice*, you never know when God will come looking for his pound of flesh. At any moment, he may ask you for the things that mean the most to you, an object, a dream, a person, whatever. Nothing is off limits. And as you raise the knife over your head and prepare to bring it down, God's cry to 'Stop!' may never come. There may be no ram in the thicket. Or if there is, God may not be prepared to take it instead.

As this suspicion about God grows and begins to bear fruit, we begin to follow God hesitantly, unsure of what He'll want us to burn next. We may remain faithful to God, obedient (though perhaps not fully loving Him), distant from everything and everyone around us because who knows when He'll take it away. These reactions were exposed in me a few years ago when I saw a Demotivational Poster with a picture of Abraham about to bring the knife down over Isaac with the caption, "God told me to: Either God is evil or you're insane. Take your pick." Though it would be sacrilegious to say it, this is what many of us subconsciously believe. We quietly begin to question God's goodness and our sanity for following Him.

It wasn't until I heard Rob Bell's take on this in *The Gods Aren't Angry* that I was able to make peace with this passage. He raises the issue of why Abraham doesn't ask

God 'Why?' Child sacrifice is one of the most disgusting, horrific acts imaginable. How could someone just accept such a command willingly? Unless, of course, you were accustomed to such divine requests. Unless this sort of thing happened in your world. And in Abraham's world, it did.

At this point in history, religions developed and built up around attempts to please the 'gods' you depended on. A god of the sun, of fertility, of water, wind and war. The peoples surrounding Abraham would regularly make sacrifices to please these powers, offerings of livestock and the fruit of their harvest. Which was fine when things were going well. They reminded the people that they were not completely independent, they brought rhythm to the community, times of celebration and thanksgiving. But when things didn't go well, obviously your previous sacrifices were not enough. You needed to give more. But as a result of things not going well, you have less to give, less fruit of your labour. You begin to run out of things to sacrifice to a god who just will not be satisfied until eventually you are offering the only thing you have left: the fruit of your womb, your children.

Abraham doesn't ask why because he knows why. The gods are insatiable. They take what they want. He knew this might happen. He climbs the mountain and prepares to give his son because, as despicable and destructive as it is, this is nothing new.

Which, Bell argues, is exactly why God calls him to this place and this sacrifice. To stop the descent of the knife and show Abraham that he is not like other gods. He will never ask for a child to be sacrificed to Him. It's not simply an issue of whether or not God can trust Abraham, it's Abraham's opportunity to discover that he can trust God, that he will not be subject to the cruel, insatiable hearts of other gods. This God is good.

To push this somewhat controversial interpretation of this passage even further, I sometimes wonder if Abraham actually failed the test. He has already shown his faithfulness so I'm not convinced that, after 25 years of obedience, God needs more evidence. God has called Abraham to be the father of a new nation, a people that will reveal God to the world. A God who later will call Israel to abandon the Valley of Ben Hinnom as a place of shame after they sacrifice children there. A God who repeats throughout their narrative that He takes no pleasure in blood sacrifices, that He wants their hearts. The way that Abraham follows God will be how his descendants follow Him.

I wonder if God was hoping that Abraham would say no. Or at least ask why. In doing so, he would be living according to the heart of the God who reveals himself throughout the narrative of Scripture. Whether he passes or fails God's test, what's crucial is that this is God showing that He is not bloodthirsty, He is not insatiable, that His heart is good. That He can be trusted with our lives, our loves and our dreams.

The Heart of God

I remember being on a mission team when I was 18 and having a friend ask me what the rudest part of the Bible was. At this point in my life, I was sure I knew everything and realised I had no idea there even were rude or crude passages in the Bible, and responded with words that I hated then but have since come to love: 'I don't know.' She responded (gleefully, I might add), with Ezekiel 23:20: 'There she lusted after her lovers, whose genitals were like that of donkey and emissions like that of horses. So she longed for the days of the lewdness of her youth in Egypt where her bosom was caressed and her young breasts fondled.' I didn't believe her, so I looked it up and there it was. Flabbergasted, I started to read around it to see who had spoken such bile and what the inevitable punishment would be for such words, only to discover that the words were God's. They were part of a narrative flowing through Scripture where God describes himself as a forsaken lover longing for the return of his wayward wife. Soon after this, I read John Eldredge's paraphrase of the story of Hosea in *The Sacred Romance*, a story that began a transformation of my mental picture of God and my suspicions about His heart.

Hosea was a prophet bringing the words of God to the rebellious nation of Israel and, like many prophets, was given a visual task to explain a spiritual reality. Throughout the Prophets, these tasks range from the obvious to the bizarre. Jeremiah bought a field and made a pot. Ezekiel cooked food over cow dung (a compromise after he refused to cook over his own fecal matter) and Isaiah wandered naked for three years. Hosea's task is even stranger. God calls him, without explanation, to marry a prostitute. Though easier to obey than Ezekiel's and Isaiah's, Hosea's must have been the most confusing. But he obeys nonetheless, falling in love and eventually marrying a streetwalker named Gomer. And things go well for a while. They are in love; they start a family. Hosea is loving every moment until the day Gomer leaves without apology or explanation. Even worse, she has left him to return to the life that she lived before, going from bed to bed and man to man.

Two reactions vie within Hosea for his attention. On one hand, he is crushed, heartbroken and in anguish. He can't believe the one he loved, gave his life, heart and body to has walked away. She has chosen a life that will destroy her over everything that Hosea offers, and he is inconsolable. The other emotion is overwhelming, uncontainable anger at God. He confronts Him without holding back, pouring out his fury, his disappointment and his confusion.

I had a lecturer in Bible college who once told us that she questions the authenticity of anyone's faith if they haven't sworn in the face of God. I didn't know how to react to that statement, having always felt that prayer demanded my reverence and thus changed my tone and my language, causing me to prefer 'Thou' over 'You', a whisper over a shout. But, as she explained, 'If you don't tell God exactly how you feel in the words that you feel it, then you rob Him of the thing that he wants the most. Your heart.'

There are few more impacting truths I have heard than this one. It is what makes the Psalms so achingly beautiful, the poems, songs and honesty of 'a man after God's own heart,' some of which one would find difficult to read in religious company, they are so raw, honest and naked. And this is exactly what Hosea does: he holds nothing back. He basically asks God (and I'm paraphrasing here), 'What good could this serve? What possible message could be so important that you would have to communicate it through my pain and anguish? What purpose could this serve?'

And God replies, 'Before you could speak my message, you had to feel what it is like to be me. To love passionately, giving absolutely of yourself only to have this love spurned, to have your lover walk away not only from your love but into the arms of everything that will destroy her. Now, here's what I want you to do. Go and win her back. I don't care what it takes, what it costs. You do whatever it takes to bring her home because this is what I am going to do for my people.'

Hosea obeys. It is the most humiliating picture imaginable, Hosea wandering the streets of his town, knocking on doors to ask, 'Em ... is my wife in here? Is that my wife wrapped in your sheets?' Knock, knock. 'Yes, I know she cheated, I know she left but all is forgiven, it's time for her to come home.' Knock, knock. Knock, knock. Until he finds her. She has gone into debt and is a slave, so abused, taken advantage of and treated like an object that she is– as Eldredge describes her– 'barely recognizable in body or soul.'

Her owner demands all Hosea's money and half of his possessions, and Hosea, in spite of her betrayal and motivated by nothing but love, pays it, takes her home and nurses her back to health. This is how God decides to communicate His heart for His people, for us... for me. It is this story that foreshadows and explains the life, death and resurrection of Jesus for me better than any other. That he will do whatever it takes to rescue us, to free us from that which would destroy us or own us.

God Hates Sin

I was at a dating seminar a few years ago at a conference in Bulgaria where, though it didn't help me find or keep a girlfriend, I heard one of the speakers tell a story that opened my eyes to God's feelings about my life. His name was Philip, and he told his story about finding the girl of his dreams and losing her to cancer just two weeks before their planned wedding day.

We listened on the edge of our seats, our hearts in our mouths as he told of the agony of those days, the pain that has followed him since and the doubts that push in from the edges of his heart and mind on the dark nights of the soul, when it's hard to trust and hard to believe. He recounted a conversation that he had with God a few months later about his struggles with how he saw sin and God's seeming obsession with rules.

He asked, 'What's the big deal? What's with all the rules? Why do you hate sin so much?'

And God answered, 'Philip, why do you hate cancer so much?'

'Because cancer stole from me the person that I love the most.'

'Well, that's why I hate sin.'

I didn't just need a new view of the heart of God, but an insight to how God sees me and my life.

In a world where God hates sin because He loves rules, John 3:16 becomes, 'For God so loved the rules that He created people to obey them.' And I want nothing to do with that kind of God.

But if God hates sin because sin is everything that destroys me and the people around me, if every rule is a clue to the heart of God and where life can be found, then perhaps I can find my home here. Here with a God who has journeyed out to free me from foreign land and field. Home with a God who has pursued me and is always pursuing me, and has done everything possible to bring me home. Home with a God who hates everything that threatens not my morality but my very life and potential as His treasured child.

I think this is what Mother Theresa experienced. I heard about an interview with her where a journalist asked her, 'When you pray, what do you say?'

She answered, 'I don't say anything--I listen.'

'Ok... when you pray, what does God say?'

'He doesn't say anything.--He listens,' she concluded with a smile.

I think this is what home with God is like, what intimacy is all about. A communicative silence, two hearts becoming one, our lives changed by the life and heart of God. And I think this must be where the Christian life is lived. Before morality, before works, before calling, everything flows from the ever-growing experience of being at home with Him.

Chapter Seven

HEALING

This great evil ... Where's it come from?
How'd it steal into the world?
What seed, what root did it go from?
Who's doing this? Who's killing us?
Robbing us of life and light,
Mocking us with the sight of what
we might have known.
Does our rule benefit the Earth?
Does it help the grass to grow or the sun to shine?
Is this darkness in you too?
Have you passed through this night?

- Explosions in the Sky [5]

Have you passed through this night?

It's hard to fully engage with the lyrics above without the music that accompanies it, but I love this song. It's

---

[5] The words themselves are actually taken from the narration of 1998 film, The Thin Red Line, directed by Terrence Malick.

one of those songs you can't listen to in big groups or as background music, but keep to yourself for midnight walks when life won't let you sleep, when you choose to hear the cry of the world in its brokenness and add your voice to others'. If one was to make a film of the early chapters of Genesis, I would have to suggest this song for the journey of Adam and Eve as they leave Eden and face their first night in a broken world, where suddenly things aren't what they were, when all that surrounds them is a threat, after all they have ever known has been safety. When they, like us, look at their lives and ask, 'How did this happen? How did things become this messed up? How did I become this messed up?!'

They were home with God. They walked with Him in the cool of the evening, found their sustenance, their identity, their very lives in being at home with Him. And this darkness steals into the world through a lie, the words of a serpent that cause them to doubt the heart of God, to believe that He is holding out on them. What they believe to be true changes. The notion of who God is and who they are as a result—a belief upon which they have built their lives—becomes something else. It changes the way they see Him, themselves and life. So 'sin', the source of the world's brokenness and its dizzying downward spiral, is an action—but that action flows from a belief. Sin is the external expression of an inner truth. Sin is not simply an action but instead a reaction to what we believe at the deepest levels of our selves.

This is not how I was taught to understand sin as a young person in the church. I grew up believing that God was a God of rules and that being a Christian meant being obedient, following the rules without questioning, changing my lifestyle, becoming more disciplined, refraining from the bad stuff. But discipline will not repair our brokenness, restraint will not bring light to our darkness. Our lifestyles are not independent choices in need of correction, but flow from the deep places of our lives, from the wounds we have received as we seek to pass through a night that will not end, waiting for the dawn that will put us back together.

Of Messages and Mirrors

In my second year of ministry at the ripe old age of 22, myself and my boss, Jude, recruited our first gap-year team. We had four students join us to work alongside us in schools, youth groups and churches. Before we began the actual work, we journeyed to a house in the middle of nowhere to spend some time getting to know each other, learning about ourselves and hearing God's voice as to what He was calling us to for the year.

Our HR Manager, Kate, joined us on one of the mornings to help us look back at where we've come from, and at the events in our lives that have shaped us. In The Sacred Romance, Eldredge talks about the 'The Message of the Arrows,' the way that our hearts interpret the messages that we receive and how these messages alter our lives' direction.

And everything is a message. It can be the simple things, like my habit of never being on time, something I couldn't have cared less about until my friend Greg told me that my lateness told him that our time together didn't matter to me. It was like a slap in the face, a message I never intended to give or even thought about... but so true. How could he feel any other way?

Or it can be the deeper things, wounds we receive from the way our parents treated us, from breakups or gossip, from mistreatment, neglect or abuse. All the words and actions of others toward us, the words spoken about us, the choices that we make, all act like a potter's hands applying pressure to wet clay, shaping us as we become harder and harder and eventually drying, becoming the product of these messages unless something sets us free.

So I was delighted that Kate came to lead us through this because I felt this was what the students really needed; I had no idea what God had in store for me that day. During a time of reflection, I started to draw pictures of myself in reality and the things that I saw in the mirror when I looked at myself, visual realities (about my insecurities) and character realities (visible only to myself). When the time came for us to share what we had learned, I couldn't hold back the tears. They came in a torrent as the veil was pulled back on what had always been true but I had never known about myself.

I had thought my life was a process of actions and choices that were sinful and dirty in my dark moments, my life lived in disobedience to what my head believed to be true. In fact, the opposite was true: my life was a series of reactions to what my heart believed to be the reality of who I was. The lies I had spent my life unconsciously believing owned me, shaped me and defined my life's trajectory.

I would have loved to be able to write this chapter through the stories of others affected by their pasts, but that would rob both you as the reader and me as the storyteller. You would be hearing the stories of those not present, told secondhand by one who never experienced them. And I would be robbing myself of the healing that comes from telling my own story, from opening the doors to the dark rooms and corners of my life that for too long I have thought I should hide.

I have to remind myself that I am called to be real, be honest, be authentic about who I've been, who I am and who I'm becoming. And it's not the story in itself that's difficult; church has taught me to tell my story and talk about how God has changed my life. If this story was completely resolved, it would be an easy story to tell. But the fact that my wounds and my brokenness are constantly raising their ugly heads in my life makes it hard because this story is not over. I am not completely healed nor am I completely whole, and I'm not sure that I ever will be this side of home.

My Story

I was cursed in my teenage years with one of what I feel must be the worst blights that could befall a boy becoming a man, and that was that I wasn't. I was a 'late-bloomer' and didn't really start growing (whether that be height or hair) until I was 16 or 17.

If you saw me writing now, you would see my face adorned with a bushy beard that I sometimes think is a raised middle finger to my past; that I have become a man in spite of my rocky beginnings. But I had no need to shave until I was 20. In my international high school in Bangladesh, I was the eternal boy, surrounded by boy-men in various stages of development, all of whom had a serious head start. This did not go unnoticed by those around me, and there was nothing in my life that I was more conscious of than this particular failing that I could do nothing about. Like so many things for so many teenagers who struggle for the control that adolescence promises but rarely delivers, it was out of my hands.

I see now, as I couldn't then, that everyone around me-- particularly those who looked the strongest--were fighting the same battle and struggling with the same brokenness. Two guys in particular I will never forget because they entwined their story with mine. They both were struggling with addictions and losing control in their fight for it. I don't know what drove them to their addictions, but I can recognise now that these were just symptoms of the brokenness that they were unable to overcome, as were their actions towards me when I was 14 and 15.

Every day I would come into school to my first class, PE, which I shared with these two guys, even though they were a couple of years ahead of me. They were angry in a way that they could not contain and would take it out on everyone around them. Somehow I caught their eye, an easy target, smaller, weaker and more insecure than everyone else, and I become their release.

The abuse began as verbal but soon moved to physical violence. A fist would fly through my shower curtain. I would be pushed around or wedgied. Each day held a different torment and I struggle to remember every event that happened over that time. I have told this story many times since, and I struggle to remember clearly, unsure of just how much really happened, and how much of it is exaggerated in my memory by my fear, my hurt or my anger. I don't know if I need it to be bigger than it was in order to justify the ways in which it crushed and broke me. But what I do remember clearly is the fear that going to school held for me, the anger at them tied with the longing to be accepted by them, the dreams before sleep of avenging myself or becoming one who would not be bullied because I was worth more than that.

Every insult, every punch, every wedgie was a message that I came to believe: that I was worthless, insignificant and would never be a man. I came to see masculinity as something that had four criteria (as we often simplify things in our youth). A man was big (which I wasn't), strong (struck out again), hairy (definitely not) and good at sports, my last hope of, if not being a man, then at least appearing to be one.

So I tried out for every team going. I didn't get on to the basketball team, was an alternate on the volleyball and track teams, and made the first team for the swim team and eventually the football team.

The football team was a coup that I had been dreaming of for years as it was the sport I loved the most and was populated by the guys to whom I had handed the power to tell me who I was. I was the smallest and youngest player on the team and hoped beyond hope that this would be my inroad to the popularity I dreamed of or the acceptance that I would settle for. But it was not to be.

One afternoon, after training ended, the team was showering and I came from the showers into the changing room wearing a towel, dreading getting dressed in my subtle routine to avoid displaying my lack of manhood to the men that surrounded me. As I came back to the lockers, my usual bullies and two other guys grabbed me, pulled off my towel, hit me and knocked me over in front of the whole team. This moment is the most crushing memory, one that I blocked out of my mind until God brought it back to me in worship one night and spoke of the brokenness that has haunted me since then. I heard two messages. From the guys who did the deed, I heard, 'You will never be a man or be accepted by us.' From those who stood at the side, watched and did nothing, some of whom were friends, I heard, 'You will always be alone; no one will ever stand beside you or defend you.' I feel like most of my life since then has been a reaction to this moment, one of the most heartbreaking events in my life.

I have told this story many times in my work in schools, and it's somewhere in the middle of what most people experience. Some cannot relate because their experiences have been more extreme––rape or abandonment or any of a number of things that so tragically befall teenagers today. Others feel guilty about their brokenness because their experiences don't seem as obvious or severe; the messages they have received feel insignificant in comparison.

But there is no Richter scale for the earthquakes that shake our lives. Some will recover from what seems the most life-shattering events, others will be unable to dismiss the echoes of words spoken to them or about them. We are all broken. We are all hurting. Our lives and hurts cannot be compared against each other. They can only be understood in terms of the damage that each message or blow has wreaked upon our hearts. They can only be measured by how they have altered our paths away from our potential and pushed us towards a life of reaction where we wonder if we will ever be able to regain control.

The illustrations you see on these pages show how these events have altered my emotional response to my reflection in the mirror. The first depicts my size and my inability to see myself as anything but small. I am now just over six feet tall--I am no giant, but taller than those who bullied me. But my experiences meant that up until a couple years ago, I would walk down the street and see myself as smaller than everyone around me, no matter how much taller than them I was. So many experiences change not only our understanding of our value, but extend even further to our physical understanding and perspective of ourselves.

Added to this was my heartbreak at being unable to defend myself. I was weak physically but also came to believe that I was weak in character, that I would always follow and never lead, always be influenced and never influence others. I believed that I was insignificant, invisible and dependent on everyone around me.

As Eldredge says, with every message or arrow we receive, we make a vow, a promise to ourselves about how we will live in the face of what we have been through. My vow was to never allow men to tell me who I was. I would turn instead to girls: surely if they accepted me and loved me, then I would be worth something. I watched romantic comedies and listened to what girls said they wanted in a boyfriend and went under a radical personality transformation, changing everything that was unacceptable, learning the right words, the right actions and the right emotions to manipulate a girl into falling for me, living off her affection and attention until I got bored and unsatisfied and moved on to the next conquest. I moved away from all my male friends and became part of a group of girls, all of whom I would date or make out with, every touch, look, commitment or kiss a message telling me I was worth something.

There is a fascinating sociological principle called the 'Looking Glass' self, the idea that we only ever see ourselves as worth the value given to us by the most important person in our lives. For me, it began with men, and their words and actions broke me. I removed the priority that I put on them after I could take no more, placing it on my girlfriends instead, and though this acted as a Band-Aid on the wound, their affection became an addiction rather than an antidote. So I went from girl to girl and relationship to relationship, never truly with the other person because no matter how intense my feelings, at the deepest levels of my heart, women were objects to me, syringes of worth to satisfy my hunger and meet my needs. Every time I entered a relationship, I would end up hurting the person that I was with, never truly intimate, never truly giving of myself but instead using her up. I gained a reputation as a heartbreaker, as one who couldn't be trusted, who could never make it work, who would always hurt.

This explains the next mirror. In reality, I hold out my heart, but in the reflection I hold a knife, because whenever I got involved with a girl, she was always going to be wounded by me. I look back over my relationship history with a lot of shame and though forgiven by God, I struggle to forgive myself for the choices that I have made.

The fourth mirror refers to my weight. When I was 12 or 13, I started eating voraciously, as if storing up energy for the growth spurt that would happen five years later. To those closest to me, it was incredible: it seemed that I could eat anything and not put on any

weight, often cleaning the plates of others after finishing my second helping! I earned the nickname "fat boy" because I ate huge amounts but it never showed, which made people feel comfortable joking about it. But sometimes, the jokes that are made about us because we are not the name they have called us, become our reality. We begin to think, 'Why would they say that if it weren't the first thing that comes to mind when they see me? Surely, the writer of Proverbs is

right: "From the overflow of the heart, the mouth speaks.'"
So I began to see myself as overweight in the mirror, the
jokes made about me becoming my reality.

The final mirror is my experience
of church and Christianity. On
the real side of the picture I am
walking past the mirror, but
in my reflection I leave dirty
footprints wherever I go. I have
always struggled to accept grace
and forgiveness though I am
aware of my constant need for
both. It's like the marks left on
me from the dirty and dark
places that I inhabited before my
faith became real--and in many,

many times since I started trying to follow God--have left
indelible marks that not even God can remove.

Perhaps it's more than that. Not only do I feel unable to live
free from the marks, I also see myself as a source of this
darkness, leaving the dirty footprints of my brokenness
wherever I go. My darkness follows me and flows from
me, the grace I have received acting as a cloak for my dirt
rather than purifying it.

Sickness vs. Symptoms

My account of my journey as the Prodigal Son in a previous chapter paints a picture of the things I needed to change in the church's eyes during my teenage years, but makes no sense in isolation from what was happening in my life at the time. What we as Christians have a tendency to label as sin is often just the visible growth of the weeds in the soil of our lives, but we often pay little or no attention to the roots that exist at a deeper level. So we run our lifestyle lawnmowers over their growth more and more regularly, only to have it grow back faster and stronger because they haven't been pulled by the root that this darkness sprouts from. The temptation is to treat sin as the sickness when it's really just the symptom.

I was 13 the first time I was caught smoking by my parents. My cousin had somehow convinced me that we could get away with smoking in my Granny's bathroom; I have no idea why I believed him, and when my mum questioned me, I knew it was time to own up. I couldn't hide any longer so I let everything out, telling her about my choices to smoke and drink over the previous year. She was absolutely crushed. We were at home in Ireland on holiday at the time, and I begged her not to tell my dad, but she told me she had to, and so I lived in fear for the next two weeks as I waited for him to return from Bangladesh. After my mum told him, he approached me and told me to get in the car, that we were going somewhere.

I was terrified. It was hard enough dealing with my mum's disappointment, but I thought my dad wasn't going to be a soft touch, that he was going to be angry. So I got into the car, with no idea where we were going and not quite convinced that he wasn't going to kill me and bury me in the woods.

Fear can do strange things to a person. It can cause him or her to question things that should never be questioned. I was so afraid and ashamed that I forgot my dad's heart, assuming he would tend towards punishment, not because of who he is but because of my own perception of what I deserved.

He got into the car and drove us to a hotel where he brought me inside to the restaurant and bought me dinner. After we got our main courses, he finally broached the subject and asked me a simple question: 'Why?'

He wasn't angry that I had broken the family rules, he was scared. Scared of the choices I was making, the dangers that I was putting myself in the path of, the things that would drive me to drink at every opportunity I could find. At that dinner, my Dad bestowed dignity on me, let me know that I could make my own decisions but that he wanted me to promise not to drink anymore. But more importantly, he let me know that if I ever broke that promise, that he never wanted me to hide these things from him and my mum, that I could always come to them and be honest.

And I did break that promise. Many times. I didn't live in fear of them, but I did continue to hide things––not out of fear, but out of shame, and because it was too hard for me to believe that their love was strong enough to keep going when I would fall. Their love seemed too good to be true, as God's does to me so often.

That dinner with my dad taught me more about God than I ever learnt in church, though I think I'm only now coming to truly understand more than I did back then. That day, I learnt unconsciously that the 'why?' is more important than the 'what?,' that the dark things that drive us are more dangerous than their expression, that the sickness is more dangerous than the symptom.

As Christians I think we have a tendency to fight the symptoms more than the sickness. We are more concerned with not doing whatever it is that tempts us than we are with asking why we are so drawn to it, exploring the root of the darkness or brokenness in our lives that is pulling us in that direction. So we train ourselves in the don'ts, and in doing so, take aspirin to fight the headache that is the result of a brain tumour.

My struggle with alcohol was not the problem, it was just a symptom of my true sickness, my need for escape because I wanted to distract myself from my pain, my need for acceptance because others defined me, my need for the confidence that drink brought because I had no confidence in who I was. My brokenness comes out in other ways today, in seeking the same things that alcohol offered me in affirmation from my work as a speaker or affection from girls or popularity.

Like my friend Philip said, God hates sin because it steals from Him the people that He loves. Sin is not simply breaking the rules, it is the state of living out of our brokenness--this is where God wants to change us. He doesn't want simply to change our lifestyles, but to change our lives. He wants to meet us at our broken inner reality, to reveal to us the truth of who He is and who we are as a result, transforming us literally from the inside out.

Healing

The greatest truth that I have experienced over the years since acknowledging what I see in the mirror is that my experience of home with God and my experience of His healing are inextricably linked. I cannot be healed without journeying and being home with Him. I cannot truly experience home with God without experiencing the truth of His heart as a healing touch, reaching into and transforming the deepest places of brokenness in my life. And yet, I fear that we as the body of Christ, as individuals and communities, have not been taught to follow this road. I don't think I'm the only one to feel like a child of God journeying from foreign land to field, dissatisfied, broken, never truly home.

It's as simple as this: if God's character is as good as the Bible says, if God is truly the God of Hosea, if He is truly revealed in Christ, if His death and resurrection are truly the ultimate act of rescue, then this changes everything.

Because everything is a message. From stories like the Prodigal Son, we hear the voice of God calling us home, we see that God is not calling us to earn our place before Him but simply to take it. When God reveals Himself in Hosea, we hear, 'No matter how far you run, no matter how deep you fall, no matter how badly you are broken, I will come for you.' In Christ, we learn that we are worth dying for and that He is worth living for. The Bible is God's message, not a book of rules, but the truth of who He is and who we are as a result, of our value, our potential, our true reflection in the mirror.

In Jamie Tworkowski's incredible recounting of the journey to healing of his friend Renee, entitled, *To Write Love on Her Arms*, he writes:

> *'I would rather write her a song, because songs don't wait to resolve, and because songs mean so much to her. Stories wait for endings, but songs are brave things bold enough to sing when all they know is darkness. These words, like most words, will be written next to midnight, between hurricane and harbor, as both claim to save her.'*

My story and your story don't have endings. They can't be finished and published and bound so that they would become eternal, completed and never again subject to change. I can't tell you that my mirrors are gone or that I am healed, for I am not.

But I know this: I know now that my experience of home has changed me. I know that as God's voice has become louder (or perhaps my ear attuned more to it, because it seems that He prefers to speak in whispers), I am able to look in the mirror and see more of what He sees than ever before. I know that I am not a boy any more, that I am not the child I was. In my strongest moments, I know that the messages delivered to me by bullies were lies. I know that He believes that I have strength within me that can change the lives of others because it is His strength and when He uses it, rescue is possible--both my rescue and the rescue of others. I know that my weight does not define my worth, no matter what MTV or magazines tell me. I know that I will always struggle to be free of the need for affection from women and the desire to find my worth in their arms. I know that I treat women better than I ever have but not as well as I long to. And I know that when God sees me, He does not see dirty footprints following me, but light flowing from me because He put it there.

I don't need a lot of faith to believe the right doctrine or the historical truth of the Bible or that God is real; this is not the struggle of following Jesus for me. I need the faith to believe the impossible about Him, that He truly is as good as He is––and this is hard because I have never seen, heard or felt goodness like His. I cannot understand it, cannot contain it, cannot plumb its depths. I am a child of God, worth dying for, pursued, loved, liked, rescued. A child that is healed because he has found his home, standing in a room of empty mirror frames, surrounded by shattered glass, looking into the eyes of a Father in which he can just about make out his reflection, his worth defined by the look upon His face as a smile breaks across it.

To come home is to be healed.

Chapter Eight

CAUGHT KNEELING

'There is no other stream.'

- CS Lewis

Say it Like You Mean It …

Apologies are tough. I remember being furious as a kid when my parents would tell me to apologise for something I didn't feel was wrong. Standing in front of a person feigning injury, I would spit my apology through gritted teeth, furious at being so powerless. That was hard enough. But I would almost explode when my mother would follow up with, 'Say it like you mean it!' My inner monologue would scream, 'I don't mean it! It's bad enough you're making me say the words; my tone is all I have left to protest with! We all know I don't mean it! Let's just leave it at that!'

But the older we get, the better we get at faking it. At saying what's necessary to keep the peace or put the past behind us. We don't get any better at being sincere, we just get better at seeming that way.

I can't tell you how many times I would have been attacked by someone if they could have heard the voices in my head while I was apologising. I don't have the space for all those stories, and I'd be mortified to recount them. The only way I can keep sane is to finish the sentences in my head:

'I'm so sorry (that you're such an idiot).'

'I really didn't mean to offend you (and your ludicrous sensibilities).'

At other times I apologise through thinly veiled translations:

'I really didn't think you'd have a problem with this' (I thought you were a reasonable, rational human being).

'I hope we can get past this' (you need to get over this).

'I think we were both in the wrong' (If you don't apologise right now I may be forced to end your ill-thought-through existence and correct God's mistake in allowing you to be here).

The more time we have to prepare an apology, the more time we have to craft our words and our tone. Which makes me more than a little sceptical about the Prodigal Son's apology, crafted in the pigsty before he makes the long walk home.

His decision to return home does not begin with, 'I can't believe what I've done to my father,' it begins with, 'I can't believe I'm considering eating pig food.' We hear no remorse, just a carefully-worded speech. There is a statement of the facts and the conditions of his return. He knows the words to get back in the door; he is willing to acknowledge that he has sinned against and hurt his father. But he is not saying he's sorry. He is not saying he regrets it.

When we use this parable as an analogy for repentance and conversion, we assume he has learnt from his destructive choices, that he is broken and consumed by remorse. But what if the only thing that he has learned is where to get food?

I'm not saying he isn't sorry or that he doesn't regret it. I just don't think it's the reason he goes home. He hasn't allowed the regrets to come flooding in, he hasn't come to terms with his own failure. His journey home is not motivated by a heavy heart but by an empty stomach. He is returning in the same way that he left.

The Prodigal Son left out of a desire to define his life. He wanted to build his own life on his father's dime. He wanted to live on his own terms without living under the family name and expectations. He returns in the same way: wanting to be able to achieve and receive without being a son. His journey is not over. It's actually continuing along the same trajectory that it always has been. He comes home to a father that he believes wants workers, not a father who misses his sons.

Some will teach on this story and say that the Prodigal Son's issue or sin is rebellion. Quit rebelling and come home. Fall in line. Follow the rules. Do what's expected.

But his rebellion is not his sickness, it is a symptom––his issue is control. He doesn't want to be his brother, working every minute of the day to earn the love he already has. He doesn't want to become like the father he doesn't understand. He wants to control the world around him and his place in it. And so do I.

Many people saw me as the Prodigal Son when I was a teenager and diagnosed my problem as rebellion. They saw me squandering my life on wild living in places they'd never been and said, 'That guy just needs to sort his life out. Quit rebelling and come back to church.' But every part of my 'wild living' was me trying to find the answer to a question.

Wild Living is Safe Living

Alcohol has never been the problem itself. When I hated being me, I would drink to become someone else. It helped me be the outgoing guy I wanted to appear. It took away my inhibitions and my conscience. Got me in with the people I believed had the answers to who I was and what I was worth. It dulled the pain of being bullied and of my own self-hatred. It quieted my frantic and often terrified heart. Alcohol was what I hoped would be the solution to the problem. The problem was being me and being unable to change that. It gave me the chance to control my pain. Some say it's wild; I said it was survival.

Drink led to girls in the best way I could imagine because it gave me the confidence to be someone else. Drink would take away the butterflies, the nervousness, the beauty and intimacy of a physical entanglement so that I would never have to be exposed and was less likely to be rejected. It gave me the confidence to go in for the kiss I believed no sober person would ever want, along with the excuse, if I failed, that it was just a drunken mistake. No strings, no consequences, safer than the alternative. It dulls both the pleasure and the risk of whole-hearted experience. It gave me the chance to control my fear. Some say it's wild; I said it was self-preservation.

Porn is not tempting because of the opportunity it offers our eyes, but the opportunity it offers our hearts. Sexual stimulation, domination, control and power without the possibility of rejection, exposure and being found wanting. Pleasure without exposure, seeing without being seen. She can't look through the screen and see me for who I am. It may reduce a loving, intimate act to a selfish, solo encounter but at least I can control it. Some say it's wild; I said it was safe.

Gambling at back-room poker tables made me the protagonist in a story where all I could lose was money. What makes me a bad poker player is that I tend to believe that I'm watching a film about me winning, not a game of skill and chance where others may take me down. I can risk all the money I have and feel the excitement and adrenaline of the risk without necessarily having to show my cards. No one needs to see that they weren't worth betting on-- and that's my deepest fear, that I'm not worth betting on. At least at the tables, no one has to see my cards unless I'm sure of them. I don't have to be exposed. I can control the cards I show and the cards I don't. Some say it's wild; I said it was better to lose all my money at the tables than lose everything else betting on me in the real world.

Standing up at the front and preaching passionately can seem courageous and, at the best of times, it is. But it can also be a way of hiding in plain sight. When you see me up the front, you're less likely to think I'm human, that I struggle and that I fail. You're more likely to put me on a pedestal, less likely to ask me tough questions, to challenge me or see my darkness. From the front, I can control what you see. From a distance, I can hide my faults and control your perception. I can stop you from seeing me fully, from knowing me and knowing that I am not enough.

Wild living in foreign lands has never been the problem. It's always been a pursuit of the solution. To not being enough. To being me and being unable to change that. So, like the Prodigal, I will come home safely. Who knows for how long. But it will be on my terms. I will tell you whether or not I am a son or a servant. I will control my place, my image, my value. I will control what you see so that you don't find me wanting.

Caught Kneeling

The Prodigal Son's journey home is something that plays on a loop in my head. The son walking through lands where he is a stranger back to a place where he is known. Just another person passing through town, but the closer he gets, the more I imagine people started to recognise him. To look up from their work as he passes by. To whisper to the person next to them, 'Isn't that the boy who asked for his inheritance? The one who left and spent it all? Look at his ragged clothing and the dirt on his face! Is he going home?'

I imagine more people gathering, their whispering getting louder, a crowd beginning to follow at a distance to see what will happen. Their judging eyes and words becoming a physical burden on his back, weighing him down, causing him to lower his eyes and publicly carry his shame. I imagine his anger at them and at himself. For the first time, he has had to come face to face with what he has done. It's one thing to think about something on your bed in a foreign land where it's theoretical and detached. It's a very different thing here on the road. Whispered words and judging eyes speak the fullness of the pain he has caused. Fear of what awaits him begins to build. All he wants is to get to his father's house and say what he needs to say. To get out into the fields where he can work his way back into food and shelter. Humiliated, ashamed, he trudges on.

He sees his home in the distance, looming large like a gallows in silhouette. His father runs out to meet him. His stomach turns as his father gets close enough to see what he has become, and the son begins to drop to his knees. His practiced words begin to fall from his lips but with a meaning and sincerity he did not expect. He begins to speak as his own judge, jury and executioner: 'I have sinned against Heaven and against you. I am no longer worthy to be called your son.'

But just as gravity begins to take hold and he is falling to his knees, he is caught by his father's embrace. His father's arms hold him up before he hits the dirt. The father interrupts his descent. A servant's place is on his knees. A son's place is in his father's arms. The son wants to be on his knees. From there he can define himself. He can name his sin, be convicted of his past and say what he is worth and what he deserves: 'I am not worthy to be called your son. Make me like one of your hired hands.'

The Prodigal's life is not transformed when he leaves the pigsty; it is transformed here on the fringe of his father's estate. He is the same man who left. Struggling for control, for self-definition, for a place in the world that he can earn, own and justify. Transformation comes when he is caught kneeling.

Transformation comes when we are caught kneeling. When we allow the Father to interrupt our descent. When, in the face of our cries and protestations and self-accusations, our Father says, 'Just shut up. I will no longer let you try and tell me who you are. You can't control this love. You can't earn it. You can't lose it.'

I can only imagine the tears that begin to stream down the Prodigal's face when they fetch the ring, the robe and the sandals. I can imagine him protesting as they try to clothe him in his true identity until eventually he surrenders, breaking down, giving up his ability to tell the world who he is and what he's worth.

This is my greatest struggle: abandoning my right to control my own identity. Dying to the rules of the world that tell me I am only enough when I am the fastest, strongest, smartest and easiest on the eye. Foreign lands and fields are attractive because I can achieve there. I can place myself on the map in relation to others. I know where I stand even if the standards are impossible or meaningless.

Being caught kneeling is hard because I cannot take such lavish grace. Give me rules, give me a social ladder to climb, a mirror to compare myself to others, a list of successes and failures. Give me anything but this: a grace I cannot control, a place I cannot earn, a love I cannot lose.

The Circle of Stones

Most of us spend our lives like the woman caught in adultery who is dragged before Jesus by the religious leaders in John 8. She is caught in the act and exposed, dragged from her place of secret sin into the middle of a bloodthirsty mob. They call out insults. They glare at her half-naked body. The religious leaders blame her and 'sinners' like her for God's silence. They call her the reason that God won't answer their prayers. She is tossed unceremoniously in front of Jesus, her clothes too small to cover her head and feet at the same time, the eyes of her accusers like a cold breeze that she can't escape.

Though guilty and in the wrong, she is not the point here. She is the bait in a trap they set for Jesus. Religion is at its most disgusting when people become pawns in our power games. She is a means to an end, more sinned against than sinning. Her story and her heart are unimportant to her accusers. She is the scapegoat for a religious system so corrupt that they would not recognise God's voice if He came down in flesh and talked to them. As He is in that very moment.

The mob stand with stones in their white-knuckled hands, impatiently waiting for permission to throw them with all the anger and hatred that they can muster. The religious leaders lay out their trap. Should we stone her? If you say yes, the Romans will kill you. If you say no, then surely you do not obey the Law of Moses and prove yourself to be a false teacher. They think they have him. Both answers condemn him. Finally they can be rid of this jumped-up impostor.

In the middle of a crowd looking for an excuse for violence, religious leaders stand smugly, disciples silently panic and a woman waits anxiously to hear her fate. Jesus bends down and starts writing in the sand with His finger. He looks up and says, 'Let anyone among you who is without sin be the first to throw a stone at her.' And he goes back to writing.

What was he writing?! This passage drives me nuts. It will be my first question if and when I get to Heaven. Was it laws that some of them had broken? Was it a list of the mistresses of those present? Or was it simply, 'two thousand years from now, this is really going to annoy a guy called Scott'?

I'm desperate to know because it is the combination of what He says and what He writes that causes the mob to disperse, to drop their stones, to be disarmed and disempowered of their ability to judge. It leaves Jesus and a half-naked woman and a circle of stones. The voices of judgment that have found her wanting have been silenced. The stones of condemnation have fallen from their hands, now markers of where her accusers stood, places vacant in the presence of the only one whose voice can define her. And us.

Jesus looks up and asks, 'Does no one condemn you?'

She replies, 'No-one, sir.'

You can almost hear her sigh of relief. It's over. They don't define me. They have no power over me.

'Neither do I. Now go and leave your life of sin.'

Sadly, this response was a stumbling block to me for many years. When I believed that God was quick to anger and rules-obsessed, this sounded like, 'I'm letting you off the hook this once but don't let me catch you again.' It sounded like a brief respite from punishment rather than a person being set free.

But if sin is everything that destroys us, then what He is saying is, 'I don't condemn. But leave this life that will destroy you.' He is setting her free from her past and giving her a chance at a future that is healthy and whole. He is offering an invitation to stop living in ways that will ruin her, to defy the voices that she believes define her.

Spiritual Disciplines

I am not good at doing the Christian 'quiet time' thing. I don't have a prayer list, I don't have a book of devotionals, I don't have a Bible-reading plan. Most of my spiritual life involves me experiencing these two stories as the prodigal sons and the woman caught in adultery.

Coming home to a Father I have misunderstood. Trying to get to my knees to tell Him I'm not worthy to be a son because of my failures. Trying to get to my knees like the older son so that I can show Him the fruit of all my hard work in the field. Having Him interrupt my descent, catching me kneeling and reminding me who I am. Telling me to shut up. Telling my frantic, fearful heart to be still because I am home and life is found here at His feet.

Finding myself in the circle of my accusers. The voices that shout that I am too short and too weak to make a difference in this world. The voices that tell me I'm too fat to be attractive. The voices that tell me I am toxic and will always hurt the people around me. The voices that scream that I am guilty of too much to be redeemed. That I will be the one who breaks Jesus and pushes His forgiveness too far. I wince, waiting for the stones to come.

But instead I hear them falling to the floor and the shuffling of feet walking away. Eventually I muster the courage to look up, and I find that I am alone with Jesus in a circle of stones. The voices in my head are rendered powerless. Here and now, I can receive forgiveness. Here and now I can be healed. Here and now I can be at peace.

This is a long way from 'easy way' Christianity. So much of Christian culture could be compared to Adam and Eve trying to hide and clothe themselves in the Garden of Eden.

'I was naked. Exposed. Fully me. Warts, flaws and failures. So I hid.'

God is inviting us out from the trees. To stop hiding, stop covering up, stop pretending to be something that we're not. Stop trying to earn something we already have. Stop trying to regain something we never lost.

It requires us to become like Jill when she arrives in Narnia in CS Lewis's *The Silver Chair* and encounters Aslan for the first time:[6]

> *"Are you not thirsty?" said the Lion.*
>
> *"I'm dying of thirst", said Jill.*
>
> *"Then drink", said the Lion.*
>
> *"May I – could I – would you mind going away while I do?" said Jill.*
>
> *The Lion answered this only by a look and a very low growl. And as Jill gazed at its motionless bulk, she realized that she may as well have asked the whole mountain to move aside for her convenience.*
>
> *The delicious rippling noise of the stream was driving her nearly frantic.*
>
> *"Will you promise not to – do anything to me, if I do come?", said Jill.*
>
> *"I make no promise", said the Lion.*
>
> *Jill was so thirsty now that, without noticing it, she had come a step nearer.*
>
> *"Do you eat girls?", she said.*

[6] I owe my mentor, Greg Fromholz, a massive debt of gratitude for opening up this passage and others to me. In the best way possible, it has been among the least of his contributions to my life.

"I have swallowed up girls and boys, women and men, kings and emperors, cities and realms", said the Lion. It didn't say this as if it were boasting, nor as if it were sorry, nor as if it were angry.

It just said it.

"I daren't come and drink", said Jill.

"Then you will die of thirst", said the Lion.

"Oh dear!" said Jill, coming another step nearer. "I suppose I must go and look for another stream then."

"There is no other stream," said the Lion.

We can't drink deeply or be satisfied from the stream on our own terms. God will not be moved. He will catch us kneeling. He will interrupt our descent. He will tell us to shut up and stop trying to tell Him and the rest of the world who we are long enough to be able to hear Him whisper in our ear:

'You are my child, whom I love. I am pleased with you. I delight in you. You are made in my image. You are worth dying for. You are enough.'

Chapter Nine

Twisted Questions, Twisted Lives

I'm not the most popular youth worker in the world. Some consider my methods to be more than a little unorthodox.

Last year I showed up in a night club because that's where my graduating students were celebrating. They weren't Christian kids, just kids that I loved, and they had asked if I would come drink with them. So I went, and I had a drink.

Many of the students there were drunk, many of them were under age. I didn't alert the bar staff. I didn't tell anyone not to drink. I just hung out with them, had a bit of banter and left before things got too crazy.

I don't talk about this much because I know that it will really annoy some people. They'll argue that by being there, I'm approving of their lifestyle and their choices, that I'm setting a bad example and that I'm compromising my integrity.

I can see what they mean--I really do understand their perspective. But if you ask any of the kids there that night if I approved of drunken behaviour, I know that they'd say no. They know me better than that because we've talked at length in coffee shops and drop-in centres about my feelings on substance abuse. What was important to me is that there was a party happening. It was a time where the kids I love were celebrating something huge in their lives, a massive change, a coming of age. And my options were to be there or not be there.

I couldn't control what happened that night whether I was there or not. But I could be there for a while to love on people so that if they needed help or to talk the morning after, they would know who to come to.

And I also know that the time when these kids are most honest and most likely to have a conversation about the meaning of life and faith is when they aren't sober. I want to be there for that, even if there is no guarantee that they'll remember it in the morning.

It's the sort of thing that Jesus did. It's why He was mistaken for a drunk and a glutton. If you want to love broken and messy people, then you're going to have to go to broken and messy places. People will see you enter and people will see you leave--and they will come to whatever conclusion they want to. We can't control that. The only thing we can control is how much love we show.

I tell my kids about my problems. I tell them about my past and present mistakes and how I'm dealing with them because I don't want them to aspire to an artificial perfection. I want them to aspire to a pursuit of wholeness––and that, I can demonstrate. It's messy, it's raw, it's humbling, it's embarrassing––but it's real. It lets them know that I don't want them to be flawless, I want them to be honest. I want them to know that the good things in my life co-exist with the bad. I don't ever want them to say, 'I could never be like him.'

I tell my kids that under no circumstances are they to open the Bible and read it. (Bear with me, there is a method in my madness.)

Firstly, I say this in a tongue-and-cheek way; it's not an absolute instruction. Secondly, the best way to get a teenager to do anything is to tell them not to do it. Finally––and most importantly––my kids have never failed to respond in shock by asking, 'Why not?!'

My answer is that the Bible is not an easy book to understand. It is complex and messy, a mixture of poetry, prophecy and stories that can both enlighten and disturb. Taken out of context, it can be the most destructive force in the world––we see that in the history of Christianity. Without an understanding of context and nuance, it can easily be portrayed as homophobic, misogynistic and approving of genocide and any number of other atrocities. So I can encourage them that if they do decide to read it, to make sure they come to me with questions so that we can discuss and debate and not take it at first reading.

My approach may seem controversial, but my heart is for my kids to fall in love with God and understand His love and passion for them.

I don't want them believing that Jeremiah 29:11 is about them when it isn't. I don't want them to judge 'Doubting' Thomas, I want them to aspire to loving Jesus as he does. I don't want them to judge Judas, I want them to find the ways in which they are like him.

It's this humble, questioning approach to Scripture that will lead them to a Christ-like life. The biggest danger I've seen in 21st-century Christianity is an approach to Scripture that says you can take it at first glance. Because it's easy to twist Scripture to our own desires. Televangelists do it. Politicians do it. Even church leaders do it. And it results in a body of Christ that looks and acts nothing like Him.

One of the most disturbing examples of this that I've experienced was talking to someone about meeting the needs of the poor. They said it's unbiblical and pointless to try to rescue people trapped in poverty because Jesus said, 'the poor will always be with us' (John 12:8). Without taking the time and effort to explore where this statement comes from, Jesus' words can be used to justify a life that is nothing like Christ's. And so can the rest of the Bible.

There is one simple question that helps me figure out whether or not I'm understanding a passage correctly:

Does this interpretation call me to a life of self-sacrificial and painful love of those around me?

If the interpretation gives me an excuse not to love someone, then I'm missing something. If it gives me permission to choose a comfortable life at someone else's expense, then I haven't gone deep enough. If it lets me hold a grudge and not forgive, then I've probably ignored something. If it justifies a lifestyle that does not call me to treat every person I see as made in the image of God and worth dying for, then it's off. Because it's not like Jesus–– and that's the whole point.

This is the challenge I face in everything I've tried to write here: if I am made in the image of God and worth dying for, then so are you. And I am called to live towards you in a way that affirms that. A faith that calls me home to a place where I am healed is meaningless, self-help, psycho-babble spirituality if it doesn't change the way I live towards others, if it doesn't build the Kingdom of God and if it doesn't change the world.

Twisted Questions

Several of my friends thrive on awkwardness. They go out of their way to make conversations uncomfortable and mess with people's heads.

One of them told me that one of his favourite moves is to go up to a friend who is with people he doesn't know and say, "Hey man! It's great to see you? Are you still beating your wife?"

By the time his friend realises that both 'yes' and 'no' would make him publicly affirm domestic abuse, my friend has already walked away, leaving the other to an awkward silence. It's genius.

I imagine Jesus had to deal with this a lot--not this exact situation, obviously, but being confronted by people who were asking the wrong questions.

Our questions expose both our agenda and our assumptions. One cannot give the right answer to the wrong question. Answering with a 'yes' or 'no' affirms the question, which is where the issue lies.

This is another reason that Jesus often taught in parables: they go beyond the agendas and the assumptions to the heart of the issue. They make it possible to have the conversation on terms other than those of His questioners, beyond the boundaries others have set.

I've often heard the Parable of the Good Samaritan being used as a synonym for the Golden Rule: 'Do unto others as you would have done unto you.' As nice a moral as that is, it's actually kind of selfish. It doesn't challenge us to love others, it appeals to what we want for ourselves. And it's not the point that Jesus is making.

Jesus tells the parable to a lawyer who stands up to test Jesus. His question is, 'Teacher, what must I do to inherit eternal life?'

Jesus answers with a question, as all Rabbis do when they have the chance:

'What is written in the law? What do you read there?'

The lawyer answers, 'You shall love the Lord your God with all your heart, and with all your soul, and with all your strength, and with all your mind; and your neighbour as yourself.'

Jesus replies, 'You have given the right answer; do this and you will live.'

But the lawyer asks a follow-up question. Luke says that he asks it 'to justify himself.' And I can understand the temptation.

It's so tempting to find ways to justify our lifestyles, our attitudes, our prejudices and our vices, our inaction and our apathy. His question is, 'Who is my neighbour?' Simply translated, the question is 'Who does God require me to love?' Translated cynically, it's 'Who can I get away with not loving?'

Loving God with everything is intangible, so it can't be quantified or counted. But loving my neighbour is tangible--it can be witnessed and attested to. So 'Whom do I have to love?' actually means, 'How do I tick this box? What is enough?'

The parable of the Good Samaritan is an answer to the question, 'How much love is enough love? How much love will keep God happy?'

The young lawyer's life treats love as a religious obligation that he is hoping to constrain. To him it is a burden, not a pleasure.

And the lawyer's approach to love puts Jesus in a tough situation. He can say 'everyone,' but the lawyer can just walk away, having written off Jesus as unorthodox or unrealistic. Jesus' desire is to win the lawyer's heart, to move him from this oppressive religious system of contractual obedience to an experience of the heart of God that changes his life. So He tells him a parable.

A man was travelling from Jersualem to Jericho when he fell into the hands of thieves who robbed him, stripped him and left him half-dead. Though the victim here is Jewish, anyone who comes upon him now could not be certain. If they would have known from his accent, he is unconscious. If they would have known from his style of dress, he now lies naked, abandoned and exposed.

From the outset, Jesus presents a victim whose identity cannot be determined. The lawyer and the rest of Jesus' audience would have understood this. Anyone coming upon him now would not know whether or not he was part of the group they called 'my neighbour'.

Among the listeners, some defined their neighbour as 'faithful religious Jews', those who have not fallen away from God. Others said anyone who is Jewish is your neighbour. But in the complex religious and political climate of the time, no one would have considered a Samaritan their neighbour.

And yet here the victim lies, a man who could be anyone from a Jewish priest to a Samaritan sinner. He has been stripped of wealth, identity and almost life. Any traveller would know that he is hurt and needs help. Jesus has undone the religious formula that the lawyer seeks to apply to his life by presenting a victim he can't categorise, a person in need that can't be put in a box.

First a priest, then a Levite, find the man on the road. They see him and the state that he's in and they cross to the other side of the road.

If you've ever heard this moment applied as a message about stopping to help people with a flat tyre, you've heard a teacher who has completely missed the point. Both the priest and the Levite face a deep religious question when they find the man: 'Which laws are most important to obey if I am to inherit life?'

On one hand, they are called to love their neighbour and they don't know if this man is a neighbour or not. They can't assume he's not a neighbour and, therefore, cannot overlook their responsibility to help him without breaking the law. But if they do help him, then they risk breaking the purity laws for priests.

Leviticus 21:1-4 states that priests become 'unclean' if they touch a dead body. And if you're unclean, you can't serve in the temple. Which creates a tension. Because to check if the man is alive means coming close enough to be contaminated if he's dead. No matter what they do, they risk breaking one of these laws. They have to figure out which one is most important, to them and to God. Their pursuit of holiness means not touching the dead and the dying for fear of contamination. Holiness is leaving the man to die. The God they follow prefers the clean hands of neglect to the dirty hands of heroism.

So they pass by the man, crossing to the other side of the road. From what I've heard, this description is Jesus being funny; the crowd would have been in stitches because the road to Jericho on which the man lies is less than two feet wide.[7] The picture He paints in their minds is of the dressed-up priest and Levite hitching up their religious garments and venturing off-road, awkwardly climbing the slopes around the dying man so that they aren't corrupted by his brokenness.

---

[7] This insight comes from the work of Ray Vander Laan (www.followtherabbi.com) who has some really interesting perspectives on interpreting the Gospels through Jewish culture.

And Jesus' message is here in the mocking laughter of the crowd and the wincing of the lawyer. The people closest to God awkwardly climbing around the sick and the broken to preserve their cleanliness. Many in the crowd feel that this is exactly how the religious hierarchy treat them. It pokes and prods the wounds of the neglected people the leaders are called to serve. It's an incitement to revolution against a religious system that not only does not give life, but takes it away in the name of holiness.

Jesus continues, and the laughter turns into stunned silence when the Samaritan enters the story. Samaritans are the faithless, the unclean, the ones who have forgotten God, at least in the minds of those listening. They are the butt of their jokes, not paragons of virtue. They are the source of cautionary tales about getting it wrong, not role models for getting it right.

The Samaritan rushes to the wounded man, moved with pity and compassion. The dirty, unclean Samaritan touches the wounded Jew and brings healing. The touch that should defile––the touch that defies religious standards––is the touch that restores.

At this, the crowd becomes uncomfortable, particularly the young lawyer. This is not Jesus saying, 'You have the wrong answer,' this is Jesus saying, 'You are asking the wrong question.' He's not saying, 'You have come to the wrong conclusion,' He's saying, 'You're on the wrong journey.'

Jesus ends with a question: 'Which one of these men was a neighbour to the wounded man?'

The young lawyer began the conversation asking Jesus to identify who his neighbour is. In the lawyer's mind, loving your neighbour is a response to an obligation. But Jesus' question shows the Samaritan acted as a neighbour, seeking out the opportunity to serve and sacrifice. The Jewish mindset at the time saw a neighbour as a static position that you were obliged to honour. Jesus' question turns being a neighbour into a verb, into a way of living. The Samaritan doesn't care who the victim is, he doesn't have to ask if his religion permits him to help. The lawyer is so angry and ashamed that he can't even say, 'the Samaritan,' answering instead, 'the one who showed him mercy.' And Jesus responds, 'Go and do likewise.'

Stop letting your religious life get in the way of love.

Stop looking for legal technicalities that will exempt you from the call to love.

Stop asking, 'Who must I rescue?' and start asking, 'Who can I rescue?'

Stop asking, 'Who must I love?' and start asking, 'Who can I love?'

When Religion Stands in the Way of Love

As Merold Westphal has observed, 'There is an atheism which is closer to the truth than a certain kind of religion.' The Samaritan, the one considered a heretic and a sinner, understands what it means to follow God better than those who minister in God's temple. And this is not simply a first-century phenomenon.

In the church today, religion can not only stand in the way of love, it can become an excuse not to. Church leaders often talk about not being like the Pharisees, and yet in many ways, our churches subconsciously perpetuate Pharisaical values. We talk with shock and admiration from the pulpit about Jesus hanging out with prostitutes. And we have our facts right––He did. But what's truly shocking is that we still act amazed after having this knowledge available to us for two thousand years.

When we act surprised by this, we praise His grace while exposing our own lack of it. To be surprised is to be hit by something unexpected. When we don't expect Jesus to spend time with the broken and the downtrodden, we admit that if we were God with skin on, we wouldn't. And that's the issue. Because the body of Christ is supposed to be God with skin on. And for the most part, we don't spend time with the sinner and the sinful.

Taking it a step further, it shows how quick we are to judge without compassion. We talk about prostitutes and various other 'sinful' lifestyles as if they were conscious decisions made by people whose lives are packed full of options and opportunities. It's as if we believe people become prostitutes because they are too lazy to go to college or because they felt it was a good career choice for people who enjoyed sex and wanted a flexible schedule.

But in the first century, prostitution would have been-- and is for the most part now--a last resort for those who have run out of choices.

Take Mary Magdalene. She was from the town of Magdela-- hence the name--which was decimated by the Romans. Who knows how she escaped or if she was there at the time, but we can be sure that she had lost her home, her family and her community. All those who cared for her were gone. So by the time she meets Jesus, she's been selling the only thing that she has left to sell: her body. On top of the rest of her pain, the Pharisees and religious leaders blame her and her colleagues for God's seeming abandonment of Israel. But she is not the cause of Roman oppression and violence; she is both the victim and product of it. She is among the most vulnerable, the most broken, the most hurt in their society. So it's no surprise that Jesus gravitates towards her in her pain and shame.

We like to think He hung out with her in spite of her prostitution, but perhaps He hung out with her because she was a prostitute. We shouldn't be surprised that He wanted to be a part of her life; we should be surprised that He wants to be part of ours.

Shane Claiborne tells a story in the *The Irresistible Revolution* about a friend of his who told him that Jesus never hung out with prostitutes. Shane disagreed with him and pulled out his Bible to prove him wrong. But before Shane could find his proof, his friend told him that Jesus never hung out with prostitutes because He didn't call them by that name or see them through the lens of their past. They were just hurting, broken people in need of rescue. 'Prostitute' is our word for them––not His.

To follow Jesus is to take our place among the whores, the beggars, the drunks and gluttons––and to not use any of those words in our hearts as we look around at the company of saints we join. It is to die to the desire to label their lifestyles and give birth to a life that seeks to name their story. To understand with compassion how this child of light has fallen into darkness, how this child of the Whole One has become so broken.

In the words of Irish singer-songwriter Foy Vance, our call is to 'Indiscriminate Acts of Kindness':

> She came in from the cold wet
> Dropped her luggage bags
> Looked the concierge in the eye
> Said, "I need a room for the night,
> But I don't got no money.
> Would you take payment in kind?"

He said, "It's alright
I got a room here, you can share mine.
Make the bed in the morning and that'll do fine.
You can change in the bathroom,
Hang your clothes on the line."
A tear came to her eye
She thought "How could he be so kind?
How could he be so kind?"

She sat down on the bed with a needle
He said, "I'd hate to see you bleed out,
Just fetch a warm towel,
I'll sit with you 'til you're dry."
She started to cry
Said, "Why? why? why? why? why? why?"

Consider it an indiscriminate act of kindness.

She was cold turkey
He was holding her hand
She said, "I was ruined by man,
This was never in my plans.
I dreamed of men who loved me,
Together we'd see the world.
Somehow I lost myself among the insults they hurled."

"I'm sure you're a wonderful woman,
And someday there will surely be someone.
So just relax now, it's important that you're calm."
She said, "How is it you can see past me as I am?"

Consider it an indiscriminate act of kindness.

When you took your chances,
It was like you placed a bet.
And sometimes this is the reward you can get.
I was always taught
If you see someone defiled,
You should look them in the eyes and smile,
And take their hand or, better still
Take them home, home, home.

She awoke early in the morning
Made the bed, gathered up her clothes to leave
Saw the concierge curled on the settee
Said, "What you did for me was hard for me to believe."

"I was just doing what was right.
No one that knows love could leave you out there on
such a night.

If you can help someone,
Bear this in mind
And consider it an indiscriminate act of kindness."

This is the challenge of our journey of home and healing. As we come to see and experience the character of God, we begin to feel at home. We begin to spend less time in foreign lands and the field. Instead, we find our home at His feet. The more time we spend at home, the more we begin to be healed of the wounds that we were given in the other places that we searched for life.

Instead of evaluating ourselves by the reflections we see in the 'House of Mirrors' of our culture, we begin to take our value and identity from the reflection we see in His eyes and in the smile that breaks over His face when He sees us.

The longer we live at His feet, the more our hearts become tuned to His. We begin to mourn like He does for those who aren't here. Before long, we find ourselves doing what Jesus did: rising to our feet, departing our home to be our Father in the world. Spending, even squandering, our lives to bring our brothers and sisters home. Imitating the heroic nature of God, the heroic nature of our brother Jesus.

Journeying to the foreign lands of the nightclub, the brothel and the bar.

Journeying to the fields of the pulpit and the pew.

Not living like the priests and the Levites, who believe life is a white sheet we are called to keep clean.

Living like the Samaritan, who sees life as a light. And what is darkness but an absence of light?

Not living in fear of being contaminated. Living with confidence in the contagiousness of grace.

Chapter Ten

HEROISM

In the decade I've been in youth ministry, I've heard the word 'integrity' used so much that it's almost become meaningless to me. More recently, I've found myself feeling like Inigo Montoya in The Princess Bride reacting to Vizzini's use of the word 'inconceivable', my inner monologue shouting, 'You keep using that word; I do not think it means what you think it means!' Though people don't intend to, integrity is often used as a synonym for perfection, or at least the appearance of it. While some define it as 'having strong moral principles', I prefer 'the state of being whole and undivided.' Integrity is not the opposite of sinfulness; it is the opposite of hypocrisy. It means being the same person on the outside that we are on the inside.

My strategy in my own personal battle against hypocrisy was 'fake it 'til you make it.' I tried to get it right when people were watching in the hope that it would help me get it right when no one was. All it did, however, was make me ashamed of who I was in my own private darkness, ashamed at the ever-widening distance between my public and private heart.

Eventually, the burden became too much and I realised that I had it the wrong way around. So I started being the person in public that I am in private. I stopped hiding my struggles with my addictions and my brokenness. I stopped pretending my spiritual life was more than it was. I owned my falls and failures.

To my surprise, I felt liberation rather than condemnation. Even more surprisingly, the more I made public who I was in private, the more my private life began to become whole––and the more I became like the person I want to be when no one is watching.

Taken as a whole, our lives often preach a different message than what we claim to believe. As John Ortberg says, 'Don't tell me what you believe. Show me how you live and I'll tell you what you believe.' How we live is what we believe. When I pretend to be something that I'm not, I may look like a good Christian, but I am actually preaching to myself that God does not love or accept me as I am. When I preach grace and hide my failures, I expose my lack of belief in grace. When I preach that God loves mercy and yet have no mercy on myself or others, I lie.

"It's not who you are on the inside.
It's what you do that defines you."

One of my favourite films from recent years is Batman Begins, director Christopher Nolan's version of the character's origin story. Forsaking Tim Burton's camp take on the comic book hero and a long way from Joel Schumacher's ridiculous corruption of the story in the mid-'90s, Nolan takes us to the dark, broken past of Batman, a man living in a broken city who refuses to believe that it is beyond redemption. Batman is a comic book hero, not a superhero. He has no super powers. He can't spin webs, he doesn't transform into a giant green smashing machine, he can't fly or shoot fire or read minds. He is just a man devastated by the death of his parents, who have left endless resources at his disposal. He is a man with a deep-seated belief that the world is not as it should be, and with a sense of responsibility to bring about transformation, to be an agent of change and of hope.

He is also, inevitably, a man with a long-time love interest, his childhood friend Rachel Dawes. Her nobility and passion drive her, as Assistant District Attorney, to fight the same fight against the systemic evils in Gotham City that breed crime and destruction. At one of my favourite moments in the film, Batman (whose real name is Bruce Wayne), in an attempt to disguise his identity, shows up at a fancy dinner with a supermodel date on each arm, playing the part of a playboy billionaire. He rants about the ridiculousness of superhero vigilantes. He buys the hotel they are eating at when the maitre d' complains about his dates swimming in the hotel water feature. He leaves his new hotel, wearing a dressing gown and with a girl on each arm, and bumps into Dawes just as he's approaching his expensive sports car. Conscious of how the situation looks, he says to her, 'What you see, this isn't who I am really am. It's not who I am on the inside.' She replies, 'Bruce, it's not who you are on the inside, it's what you do that defines you.'

I've quoted this scene many times, and I'm aware of the feelings of suspicion that it evokes within people. They fear I will say that your salvation is earned and your faith defined by the things that you do, the works that you achieve. Please hear me: I am not saying that. The grace of God cannot be earned; our salvation cannot be achieved by us. But I'm also conscious that I am guilty of using this as an excuse to allow my life to bear no evidence of what God has done for me and in me.

As with all the great films that resonate deeply, there is redemption in Batman Begins. Later in the film, mayhem breaks out in Gotham City and Dawes finds herself in danger only to be rescued by Batman. She calls out as he tries to leave her on a rooftop, 'In case you die, tell me who you are!' She is falling for the hero behind the mask. He tells her, 'It's not who I am on the inside, it's what I do that defines me.' And she knows his true identity, that this mask, this life as the caped crusader is the true Bruce Wayne. He does not define his life by what he believes, but by the ways in which what he believes define and determine how he lives.

Christendom has internally debated the issue of faith and works for the last two thousand years. Tragically, dissecting the mechanism of salvation based on Greek dualistic philosophy has separated two things that are inextricably linked. In the Jewish mindset, faith and works were two sides of the same coin. If Bruce Wayne believes that Gotham is broken but can be redeemed and yet does nothing to save it, then his belief is, at best, optimistic intellectual affirmation and, at worst, a complete betrayal of a city he claims to love. If he lives as a vigilante to serve his own ends or to redeem his own life, then it's nothing more than cathartic violence designed to sooth the soul. We call him a hero because he both believes and acts-- both loves and rescues.

This is what it means to be Christian. To be defined neither by what we believe nor what we do, but to evaluate our lives by how this belief has taken hold of us. It's what James writes about so scathingly in his epistle:

> 'Faith without works is dead. I can show you my faith by my deeds, can you show me your faith without them? You say that God is one, the central affirmation of our faith, and that's great. But even demons believe that ... and they shudder because his existence is not what

scares them, it's his action! Abraham was not considered righteous for believing what God said, he was considered righteous for acting on it! His faith was made complete by his actions! In the same way that a body is dead and lifeless without the spirit, faith is dead without deeds.'

James 2:14-24, 26[8]

What, then, is Holiness?

Holiness is not our ability to learn Bible verses, attend church or obey rules. Holiness is not perfection. Holiness is living what we believe, letting our lives become a manifestation of the God we have come to know and experience.

The pursuit of integrity is the journey of becoming the same person internally as we are externally, of learning to live what we believe. Integrity is becoming undivided people. Integrity is wholeness. Thus holiness is, simply, wholeness.

This is where the Christian journey leads us. We journey home from the foreign lands and fields where we have searched for life. At His feet, the Father's words about us become our truth. We are made in the image of God. We are worth dying for. We are loved beyond measurement or understanding. The more we learn to trust Him, the more

[8] Paraphrased here for emphasis

we begin to believe Him. The other voices in our lives that have fought to define us become ever-quieting noise as His voice takes over. His voice heals us, puts us back together, brings us closer and closer to being whole.

But we do not merely become consumers of the heart of God; we become echo chambers of that voice for the world around us. The more we believe His voice for us, the more we believe it for our neighbour. This is why God calls us to love our neighbour as ourselves––because when we love our neighbours less than ourselves, we live lives of selfish ambition and consumption. And when we love our neighbours more than ourselves, we live lives of inferiority in which acts of service perpetuate our self-hatred or need to earn love. Loving our neighbour as ourselves is wholeness and holiness. We come home. We begin to be healed. Unable to contain this experience of God, we begin to echo His voice to the world, to imitate His heroic nature that rescued us.

Freely loved, we love freely.

Rescued, we rescue.

Having found our home, we risk leaving it to bring others home, too.

Closer Still …

When this becomes our understanding of holiness, it redefines our understanding of living holy lives. We no longer obey archaic religious rules to keep a wrathful, unpredictable God happy. I have always struggled with this definition of what it means to live as a Christian, and how, for the most part, Christians are known for what they don't do. Somehow, the Christian journey has pulled many people into isolated church settings that look more like nuclear fall-out bunkers than communities, full of people waiting for Heaven. I can only suppose that this is a reaction to a misunderstanding of God.

But if our journey towards Him is making us more like Him, if it invites our lives as individuals and faith communities to become more and more guided by His character and His example in His interaction with the world, then our re-discovery of the character of God should naturally flow into a re-definition of what it means to follow Him.

Growing up as a young person in the church, most of what I heard about Christianity concerned my lifestyle. My Christian education focused primarily on telling me what was right and what was wrong. It was wrong to drink, smoke, do drugs, swear, have sex, shout, get angry, gossip and dress provocatively. The impression that I got was that, once I could avoid these things, all God would require of my life as a Christian would be slight tweakings--but, for the most part, I would be OK. Yes, there were things that I was encouraged to be--I should be loving, accepting, try not to be judgmental and, above all, nice--but these were all add-ons to a life based on not doing the other stuff. The Christian life was a life of avoidance, of fleeing from sin, defined more by what it was against than what it was for. It felt like being a soldier in World War II before I would climb out of the trenches to cross the 'no-man's land' of this world. I was not handed a map that showed me a path to a destination, I was handed a map of a minefield that told me where not to step rather than what to pursue.

Over the last few years, however, I've become convinced that following Christ is about pursuing, not avoiding. It's about pursuing my potential to be the man that God dreams I would be. It's about who I'm becoming, rather than what I'm not doing. In the words of Rob Bell's counsellor as Bell was struggling with the countless, conflicting demands on his life as a pastor, 'You have one task and that is the relentless pursuit of who God made you to be.' As it happens, this pursuit leads us away from the things that threaten to destroy us but it is not defined by them. The difference is subtle, yet dramatic. It leads us beyond simple questions of right and wrong--'What should I not be doing?'--into deeper questions like, 'Who am I becoming?'

This is why I generally dislike it when people label certain behaviours as 'right' or 'wrong'. It's not that these descriptions are not apt, I just don't feel that they help. For example, it's clear from the Ten Commandments that we should not steal. It's not right to steal. It's wrong to steal. But if we stop our discussion here and move on to the next commandment, then we rob ourselves of what God, in this commandment, is teaching us about life, about His heart and about what it means to follow Him.

There is a reason behind every commandment––they are not simply boxes to be ticked, but clues to a deeper understanding of God. As Christ says, we must become more like children, and with children, 'Do not ...' is not enough. They ask 'Why?' 'Why is the sky blue?' 'Why do seeds become such big trees?' 'Why should I not punch my sister?' 'Why shouldn't I poke the dog with a stick?' And if we ask, 'Why should we not steal?' then we learn something about God––possibly many things.

If I steal something, it's an external expression of several internal truths. Firstly, stealing says that I am not satisfied with what I have. Secondly, it says I care more about material accumulation than I do about my relationship with the one that I have stolen from. I am prepared to break a friendship or leave someone without so that I may have more. Perhaps we could even go as far to say that somebody who steals believes that life is about what you own––and this is an anathema to the Kingdom of God.

To steal, then, is to live inconsistently with what we believe to be true, and, by doing it, we are journeying farther from who God calls us to be.

One might then choose not to steal and so would be closer to who God calls them to be. But one may go even further and reject a life of material accumulation and instead view everything that they own as resources to be shared with those around them, particularly those in need and, in so doing, journey closer still.

When we approach the commandments and laws like this, we seek to imitate a God that we love rather than protect ourselves from a God we fear.

And the more I base my lifestyle and my discipleship of young leaders on going 'closer still', the more we feel both liberated and fully alive.

When we talk about masturbation, we stop debating whether or not it's wrong. We start dissecting the action itself and the values it perpetuates. The conclusion that we come to together is that masturbation is to turn women into objects in our minds, to treat them as something to be used and consumed for our own needs and pleasure without ever giving of ourselves. Not only this, but the more someone––or an entire gender––becomes an object of fantasy, the more we will tend to act towards them accordingly. Lust is rooted in the same anti-Kingdom values as slavery and racism, the belief that another person is worth less than you, that it is your right to treat them as you please. Discussed like this, masturbation can be a hallmark of a life that oppresses, and we each need to identify how that works itself out in our lives. We do not ask whether the behaviour is right or wrong, we ask how it is affecting our journey to become the people we were made to be.

Since we can't have a conversation about masturbation without discussing pornography, we begin to dissect that, too. Forsaking right and wrong, we ask questions about the industry, about how it messes with our expectations. And we start wondering about the histories of the actors and actresses that have led them to make a living through porn. I tell my young people about my fear that one day, I'll see one of them in an adult film. I talk about how the more I journey closer still, the more I find myself wondering what led her to this screen with this man at this time. Was she abused? Was she abandoned? Hurt? Unloved? What has she come to believe about herself that she would find herself in that position? Rather than being an object, she becomes a person. With a heart. A story.

I don't say, 'Porn is wrong. That's why I don't watch it.' I say, 'You have no idea how hard I have to work to maintain an erection when watching porn. I have to concentrate really hard to stop her being human to me. And when I do this, it detracts from my humanity. It feels like a betrayal of who I'm made to be. It doesn't mean I don't do it, it means my desire to is beginning to wane.' To go closer still is for the people in the pornography industry to become fully human to me in a way that renders my lust flaccid. Pun intended.

The more we talk about porn and masturbation, the more we begin to talk about sex and the choices we have made or will make about it. So much of today's cultural Christianity makes an idol out of virginity and a crime out of sex as if the only time sex matters is the first time we have it. Some movements about waiting for marriage unknowingly communicate repression and avoidance to those who are virgins and condemnation and judgment to those who are not. Living on the right-wrong spectrum in the area of sexuality has, in many places, unconsciously communicated that there are right and wrong people rather than right or wrong ways of approaching sex. And while I affirm that I think that having sex before marriage is further from who God has called me to be, He is not just calling to refrain.

He is calling me closer still, to the real reason that I am a virgin in my late twenties. I don't choose this because I believe God says, 'Don't.' I choose not to have sex because I can't disconnect the emotional and spiritual side of sex from the physical. As I read what the Bible says about sex, I see it as the giving of all of oneself to another, a statement of love, commitment and intimacy. The physical nature of the intertwining and the nakedness are best experienced when there is emotional and spiritual connection and exposure of the same kind.

The Bible doesn't say, 'Don't have sex before marriage,' it says that sex is the act of marrying, of becoming one. Becoming undivided. Of giving all, seeing all, accepting all. The reason I wait to have sex is because I want to be sure that when I do, she can look into my eyes and know that I mean it. I don't want to have to hide my eyes or look away when my body is saying, 'I reveal all.' I don't want to be inwardly holding back when my body is saying, 'I give you all.'

The danger of the culturally Christian oversimplification of sex and marriage is not that it goes too far, it's that it doesn't go far enough. Just because you're married doesn't mean you and your spouse are becoming one. Just because you've been naked together doesn't mean you have revealed all of yourself. Just because you've made the promises doesn't mean you're keeping them. There are many non-Christian couples having better sex––that is more Biblical––than Christian married couples who have obeyed rules written in the Bible that are not written on their hearts.

Waiting until you're married to have broken sex that is ruined by shame, guilt or selfishness is as pleasing to God as the priest or Levite who leaves a broken man on the side of the road in order to stay pure for temple duty. It's an obedience of the law that destroys it rather than fulfilling it. To go closer still is to stop asking, 'When can I have sex?' and to start asking, 'When I have sex, will it flow from my pursuit of wholeness or be just another expression of my brokenness?'

'Closer Still' Christianity abandons oversimplification to embrace complexity. In the tension and the conflict of dialogue and the dissection of our lives, we pursue truth beyond clichés and life beyond a lifestyle. We begin to ask difficult questions about what we spend our money on and what it affirms. We stop arguing that what we're saying is right, and stay silent in order to discover what those around us are actually hearing when we say it. Rather than being critics of a world around us that doesn't claim to live according to the Christian faith, we begin to challenge the failures of our Christian culture and our own personal failures as people who do make that claim.

Terms like 'pro-life' become meaningless as political slogans but powerful as values we use to re-order our inner world. Standing against abortion in principle, we also realise that the worst place to make a stand against it is outside an abortion clinic. At that place and at that time, the only thing that we have to offer is our judgment. If we want to truly be anti-abortion, we need to live among those most at risk of considering the option; we need to live and communicate a holistic view of sexuality. The place of the Christian outside the abortion clinic is not shouting at those going in but holding and loving those coming out.

To go closer still is to acknowledge that we're not really 'pro-life' if the only type of death we're against is that of the unborn.

To be pro-life is to be anti-war, anti-poverty and anti-hunger.

To be pro-life is to fight against depression, self-harm and all causes of suicide.

To be pro-life is to refuse to live out a religion that brings condemnation, judgment, superiority, guilt and shame. Especially if it calls itself Christianity.

What, then, should I hate?

To be further from who God has called us to be is to lose ourselves in what God calls 'sin': anything that destroys us or those around us. Anything that makes us or those around less human and less alive to God's understanding of who we are. To be closer is to 'hate the sin, not the sinner.' To go closer still is to ask the same question my friend Duffy asks: 'Since when was following Jesus about figuring out what I should hate?'

Further is to ignore God's law. Closer is to try to obey it. Closer still is to long for us to have it written on our hearts in such a way that we live it unconsciously.

Further is to say, 'I have no neighbour.'

Closer is to say, 'Who is my neighbour?'

Closer still is to say, 'I call you my neighbour. I won't leave you on the road to Jericho. I won't leave you in foreign lands. I won't leave you in the fields. I have come in the name of my Father and the footsteps of my Brother to bring you home.'

Chapter Eleven

A Benediction

In a world of short cuts and oversimplification, may you encounter the risen Christ at the place of your isolation and shame. May you have the courage not to change the subject when He puts His finger on the brokenness that has brought you to the well.

In a world of slick marketing, cheesy slogans and half-truths, may you hear the challenges of the life that Jesus is calling you to and respond, 'Where else would we go? Only You have the words of life.'

In a world where the goal is the brittle maturity of those afraid to question, may you discover the dynamic childlikeness of the Kingdom of God and never stop asking, 'Why?'

In a world where belief is equated with certainty, may you learn to live like Thomas, whose love led to doubt. In a world where Judas is villainised, may you find and die to the ways in which you're crafting a Jesus that shares your agenda.

In a world that promises life in foreign lands and fields, may you have the courage to come home to the Father's feet. May you find the relentless love of the God of Hosea. Or – even better – may it find you.

When you have come home, may you be healed of the wounds that you've received along the way. May you be freed from what others have said and what they've done. From what you've said and what you've done. May you have the faith to believe that you are made in the image of God and that the cross tells you that you are worth dying for.

May you be caught kneeling in your attempt to define yourself. May He interrupt your descent and may you rise, understanding who you are and what you were made for.

May you have the grace to see the world and the people around you through God's eyes. May you stop asking, 'Who must I love?' and start asking, 'Who can I love?' May you no longer be afraid of being contaminated by the world around you, but be confident in the contagiousness of the life that God has given you.

May you discover a life beyond right and wrong. May you be freed from a life lived further from who God has called you to be. May you be unsatisfied with closer. May you always go closer still.